PENGUIN BOOKS

FACTS OF LIFE

Maureen Howard is also the author of six novels: *Not a Word About Nightingales*, *Bridgeport Bus*, *Before My Time*, *Grace Abounding*, *Expensive Habits*, and *Natural History*. *Grace Abounding* and *Expensive Habits* were both nominated for the PEN/Faulkner Award. She edited *The Penguin Book of Contemporary American Essays* (1984).

Ms. Howard has taught at a number of American universities, including Rutgers, Columbia, Princeton, University of Houston, City College, Amherst, and Yale. She is an executive vice president of the PEN American Center. She lives in New York City with her husband, the novelist and lawyer Mark Probst.

Facts of Life

by Maureen Howard

PENGUIN BOOKS

PENGUIN BOOKS
Published by the Penguin Group
Penguin Books USA Inc.,
375 Hudson Street, New York, New York 10014, U.S.A.
Penguin Books Ltd, 27 Wrights Lane,
London W8 5TZ, England
Penguin Books Australia Ltd, Ringwood,
Victoria, Australia
Penguin Books Canada Ltd, 10 Alcorn Avenue,
Toronto, Ontario, Canada M4V 3B2
Penguin Books (N.Z.) Ltd, 182–190 Wairau Road,
Auckland 10, New Zealand

Penguin Books Ltd, Registered Offices:
Harmondsworth, Middlesex, England

First published in the United States of America by
Little, Brown & Company 1978
First published in Canada by
Little, Brown & Company (Canada) Limited 1978
Published in Penguin Books by
arrangement with Little, Brown & Company 1980

3   5   7   9   10   8   6   4   2

LIBRARY OF CONGRESS CATALOGING IN PUBLICATION DATA
Howard, Maureen, 1930–
Facts of life.
Reprint of the 1st ed., published by
Little, Brown, Boston.
1. Howard, Maureen, 1930–   —Biography.
2. Novelists, American—20th century—Biography.
I. Title.
[PS3558.O8823Z465   1980]   813'.54   [B]   79-27356
ISBN 0 14 00.5500 2

Printed in the United States of America
Set in Caledonia

An excerpt from this volume has appeared in *The Hudson Review.*

For
Loretta Howard

Facts of Life

I

CULTURE

"Ah, did you once see Shelley plain," one of my mother's beloved lines, delivered on this occasion with some irony as we watched Jasper McLevy, the famed Socialist mayor of Bridgeport, climb down from his Model A Ford. "Laugh where we must, be candid where we can," was another of her lines, a truncated couplet, one of the scraps of poems, stories, jingles that she pronounced throughout the day. Like station breaks on WICC, her quotations punctuated the hours. Vacuum off: "One thing done and that done well / is a very good thing as many can tell." Out on the back stoop to take in the thick chipped bottles of unhomogenized milk, she would study the sky over Parrott Avenue — "Trust me Clara Vere de Vere from yon blue heavens above us bent . . ." George and mother and me, pressed against the sun-parlor doors watching a September hurricane play itself out. Ash cans rattling down the drive, gutters clotted with leaves, shingles flying, the rambler rose torn from its trellis whipping the cellar door. Her gentle, inappropriate crooning: "Who has seen the wind?/ Neither you nor I: / But when the trees bow down their heads, . . ."

My mother was a lady, soft-spoken, refined; alas, she was fey, fragmented. I do not know if it was always so, but when we were growing up, broken off bits of art is what we got, a touch here and there. A Lehmbruck nude clipped out of *Art News* tacked in the pantry, a green pop-eyed Sienese Madonna folded in the Fannie Farmer cookbook. She was sturdy when we were children, with high cheekbones and red hair, like a chunky Katharine Hepburn, so the fragility, the impression of fragility was all in her manner, her voice. Her attitude toward anything as specific as a pile of laundry was detached, amused. It might not be our dirty socks and underwear that she dealt with at all, but one of our picture books or a plate of cinnamon toast. As she grew older her fine red hair faded to yellow, then to white, but it was still drawn back from her face and pinned at the neck as she wore it in college. Her clothes were old but very good. And my mother—the least independent of women—always used her maiden name, her married name tacked on as though she were listing herself in her *Smith Alumnae Quarterly*. Loretta Burns Kearns. Somewhat wistful. You do remember me? Loretta Burns.

I sensed that my mother was a misfit from the first days when, dressed in a linen hat and pearls, she walked me out around the block. She was too fine for the working-class neighborhood that surrounded us. "Flower in the crannied wall/ I pluck you out of the crannies." Down Parrott Avenue around to French Street we marched, taking the air — "As I was going up the stair/ I met a man who wasn't there./ He wasn't there again today. . . ." I never knew when I was growing up whether my mother didn't have time to finish the poems what with the constant cooking, cleaning, washing, or whether this was all there was, these remnants left in her head.

To the crowded A & P we charged on a Saturday morning—ours not to make reply, ours not to reason why, ours but to do and die. If she gave us a ride back to school after lunch and the scent of spring was heavy over the schoolyard fence as the nuns filed in from the convent, my mother would sing out to us, triumphant behind the wheel of the old brown Auburn: "Come down to Kew in lilac-time. . . . And there they say, when dawn is high and all the world's a blaze of sky . . . Come down to Kew in lilac-time (it isn't far from London!)"

"There once was a molicepan who met a bumblestum. . . ." A witless ditty — it must have been hilarious in her public-speaking class at college and never failed to please at lunch or dinner. But it wasn't mere nonsense or chestnuts from the laureates she quoted. My mother had studied German and I believe been quite a serious student before life caught up with her. *"So long man strebt, er ist erlost,"* she said. As long as man strives he is saved. *"Wer reitet so spät durch Nacht und Wind?"* We were treated to disjointed lines, lots of *Faust*, some Schiller and Heine, the final watery gurglings of the Rhine maidens and, of course, *"Freude, schöner Götterfunken . . ."*

It sounded beautiful gibberish to me as did the Latin verbs she conjugated to the remote pluperfect tense, but for my mother it was to prove that she could still do it, could reel it off with ease — as naturally as an athlete doing push-ups before the flab sets in. "*Amá-veram, amáveras, amáverat.*" That was the trick my mother could do and other mothers couldn't, as well as smock my dresses by hand and overcook the meat to please my father and not speak to George when he was rotten, but be elegantly wounded, disappointed in her son, like a grieving queen.

She kept a plain brown copybook to mark down all our childhood diseases and achievements. This chronicle is of no general interest: while it is gratifying for me to know that I went to the World's Fair in 1939 with the last scabs of my chicken pox and still had a wonderful time, it is terrifying to read my first poem (age seven) about the Baby Jesus and George's loathsome moral verse (age six) — both efforts already corrupted by the worst literary traditions. "Thus should a little child be merry/ In snowy, blowy January."

We were dressed in our Sunday best and taken to the concert series at Klein Memorial Hall. My father wouldn't go near the stuff. Helen Traubel stomped onto the stage in a black tent and something like gym shoes. The Budapest Quartet, all young and buoyant, stunned us with the knowledge of their own brilliance. The Connecticut Symphony ground out their Debussy and Ravel, their sloppy Beethoven, their inevitable Gershwin jolly-up. Me and my mother and George, proud and rather excited by the grandeur we could pull off in Bridgeport. The audience — a sprinkling of local music teachers, a solid core of middle-class Jewish shopkeepers and professionals who were more sophisticated than the Irish in town, and that set of rich old ladies who stumble into concert halls all over the world, canes and diamonds, hearing aids, rumpled velvet evening capes from long ago.

We never made it to Kew where all the world's a blaze of sky, but to the first little temple of civic culture, the Klein Memorial out near Bassick High School beyond the Cadillac showroom. On those special nights we were there. The price of the tickets was something awful, but my mother wanted this for us. I ran off pictures in my head, beautiful scenery, lakes and rills, mountains and fens. I called upon the great myth that one *must* be moved. I strained, while the violins soared, for deeper finer thoughts, but it was beyond my childish endurance. I tap, tap, tapped my patent-leather pump into my brother's ankle until it drove him mad, found that I had to cough, begged to go to the water fountain and was kept in my seat by a Smith Brothers' cough drop from my mother's purse.

What did it mean to her? Was my mother full of a passionate yearning like those starved women of taste who carted their pianos across the prairie? God knows, Bridgeport was raw land in the thirties. Before my father died, she sat in perfect harmony with him in front of the Lawrence Welk show. She was lost in the old sappy songs, lost. Walled in by her vagueness, all the fragments of herself floating like the million orange, green and purple dots that formed the absurd image, the bobbing head of the lisping bandmaster. My parents took my anger as a joke. Disgust swelled from me: I was not ready for compassion.

Or did Loretta Burns know that her chance was gone and only want those ineffable finer things for me and George? Well, we sure got them. We got the whole culture kit beyond her wildest dreams. There came a day when George knew who was dancing what role in which ballet that very evening up at City Center. For the pure clean line of a particular Apollo he would leave his gray basement on St. Mark's Place—burnt-out pots, ravioli eaten cold from the can, grit in the typewriter keys. His coffee-stained translations from the Spanish and Greek littered the floor. No closets. No bathtub. Now, as an adult, my brother takes with him wherever he lives an intentional chaos that is impressive, a mock poverty. Orange crates and real Picassos. Thousands of records and books but no dishes, no curtains. Money handled like trash. Twenty-dollar bills crumpled in ashtrays, checks left to age, income tax ignored. He is quite successful really. Her boy has become a strange man, but not to himself and he is not unhappy. My brother, a middle-aged man, can come to visit (filthy jeans and Brooks Brothers blazer), take William Carlos Williams off the shelf and read a passage, rediscovered: "At our age the imagination across the sorry facts" — then tell me why it is so fine, and it *is* fine. We are grown: now I can see the poem perfectly. As we talk beneath my Greenwich Village skylight he threads his speech with lines — like our mother, of course.

While I'm split, split right down the middle, all sensibility one day, raging at the vulgarities that are packaged as art, the self-promotion everywhere, the inflated reputations. In such a mood I am unable to sit in a theater or pick up a recently written book. I am quite crazy as I begin to read in stupefying rotation — *Anna Karenina, Bleak House, Persuasion, Dubliners, St.*

Mawr, Tender Is the Night, The Wings of the Dove. I
play the Chopin Mazurkas until the needle wears out.
Drawings are the only works I can bear to look at. The
atmosphere I demand is so rarefied it is stale and I
know it.

Then again, everything is acceptable to me. In an
orgy I view the slickest movie or love story on TV, suck
in the transistor music and thrill to the glossy photographs of sumptuous salads and stews, the magnificent
bedrooms and marble baths in *House and Garden*.
Our great living junk art. The Golden Arches of Mc-
Donald's rise, glorious across the landscape, con-
tempo-monolithic, simple in concept as Stonehenge if
we could but see it. Then the nausea overtakes me in
Bloomingdale's "art gallery" or as I listen to all that
Limey Drah-ma on Public Television. Sick. I am often
sick of art.

It would never have occurred to my mother that the
finer things might be complicated for us, less than
sheer delight. She simply stopped after her children left
home. There were no more disembodied lines, not
even the favorite "Little Orphant Annie's come to our
house to stay," or "Where are you going young fellow
my lad/ On this glittering morning in May?/ I'm going
to join the colors, Dad . . ." No. She settled into
Lawrence Welk, "Double Jeopardy," Dean Martin no
less, and she had all her life been such a lady. She
read the *Bridgeport Post* and clipped the columns of
some quack who had many an uplift remedy for arthri-
tis and heart disease. She followed the news of the
Kennedys in *McCall's* magazine, until the last terrible
years when she was widowed, when the blood circu-
lated fitfully to her cold fingers and her brain. Then,

from a corner of her dwindling world, she resurrected Ibsen's *Rosmersholm* in a German translation and underlined in a new ballpoint pen the proclamations of Rebecca West, all that heroic bunkum about the future, the strength of women, and her festering spiritual love.

Mother sat on the brown velvet couch day after day, rejecting tapioca and Jell-O, smiling at the pictures in her art books like a child . . . such pretty flowers . . . all the colors . . . by some Dutchman . . . in a bouquet. The fat ladies she laughed at were Renoir's, bare bottoms by a hazy stream. Her mind skipped the shallow waters of her past like a stone. George and her own father were one man. My father — her great love whom she had married against all opposition — now, my father was merely "that fellow" and there was a photo she found of Loretta Burns with a whole band of robust Smith girls, each one warmly recalled, who'd gone hiking up Mount Tom on a fine autumn day in her sophomore year. Sometimes she could not place me and so she entertained me graciously, gave me pieces of crust and cake. She was tiny now, nestled in the couch. Her thoughts fluttered away from her: "By the shores of Gitche Gumee,/ By the shining Big-Sea-Water," she said. Gaily she'd recite her most cherished lines of Heine:

> *Ich weiss nicht was soll es bedeuten*
> *Dass ich so traurig bin . . .*

What does it mean that I am so sad? She seemed happy to remember the words at all.

My Life in Art

"OH, THE IRISH" — my mother patronized her own. Too much love and exasperation was learned at her knee: the Irish — the whole insufferable lot of them — crass, low in their tastes but what could you really say against them — crooked politicians and venal priests, alcoholic virgins tottering to Mass. They were charming. We were taught to take the Irish lightly. In our house high seriousness was never the order of the day.

As kids in grammar school we said — "Well, that's the Irish" — when the nuns sent us home with books of chances on the Buick sedan, when the new Stations of the Cross were more lurid than the old. Later, when I came as a visitor to town I presumed at once that it was some thick mick mayor, true to form, who had destroyed the Victorian Gothic mansion, a dream of grandeur set in a vast garden on Golden Hill Street. I've come across that house, the Wheeler Mansion, in books on American architecture. The Metropolitan Museum took slides of every room before it was leveled. Bridgeport, a vaudeville joke of a town, had little and it opted for less. None of this seemed funny anymore: the arrogance of the mayor's sleazy taste, the hatred it implied of our meager heritage, his disdain for the duped Yankee millionaire who'd left his prized home to the citizens of Bridgeport. True, many of the fine houses in Ireland were burned to the ground after 1916 — the wrath of those people, getting back their own — but the vengeance here was petty, trashed down by the Republican City Council. It was 1958.

Joe McCarthy was still a great favorite of the *Bridgeport Post*. Who needed professors from out of town taking notes on an old house? Who needed gargoyles and turrets, pictures, rugs, copper beeches with a hundred years' growth? The Wheeler land was to stand empty for years, a useless punishment to the town. After my diatribe against the Irish my father said: "The new mayor is Italian."

This only increased my fury. "Well then," I cried, "it's Bridgeport, pure Bridgeport."

Our family was alone in the parish, mocking the world we came from — the tap routines and accordion music on Saint Patrick's night, the *Catholic Messenger* with its simpering parables of sacrifice, its weekly photos of saintly missionaries and their flock of mocha children with souls like ours, rescued for eternity. My parents were good Catholics and never meant us to find our religion a farce. It was as perfect to them as to any knee-bobbing, bead-telling spinster. The Catholic Church with its foreshortened American history and tangled puritanical roots was as inviolate to my mother and father as it was to the last-ditch aristocrats of Evelyn Waugh.

Mass, Communion, fish on Fridays, the Legion of Decency, were all part of our life. The Holy Days were honored. Belief without question: observation without piety. Once during Lent — it must have been after a scalding sermon condemning our wanton modern pleasures, so few in the thirties (radio programs, a Saturday matinee, an evening of cards) — we knelt together in the living room and attempted the family rosary. My father, playing up his role, intoning the

Aves as he'd learned them in the seminary, mother
backing him in a whisper, George and me mumbling
after. By the time we got up from the floor, stiff with
embarrassment, we all knew that charade would never
be repeated. But we set out the crèche with solemnity
at Christmas and the week before Easter the palms
were dutifully carried home from church and wound
round the finial of the dresser mirror to gather dust.
Religion was a serious business, but the Irish were fair
game. In laughing at them we laughed at ourselves,
didn't we, Catholics in good standing, pure potato-
famine Irish, gone fine with our cut glass and linens
from McCutcheon's.

Our piano lessons, taught by Sister Mary Patronella,
a large woman who dosed with Listerine so that she
might breathe freely over her pupils, cost fifty cents an
hour and were not worth the price. Then ballet for
me, elocution, clarinet for George—none of my
mother's efforts to spring us from our cultural poverty
or the dim children in our neighborhood came to
much. She found extraordinary people to widen our
horizons. A distraught mother (with a house full of
waifs in undershirts gnawing at pieces of Bond Bread)
instructed us in drawing and watercolors. Shading,
outline, perspective: the point of each academic exercise was lost in the woman's confusion: our studio her
kitchen table, old jelly jars to dip our brushes, chipped
saucers to mix our colors and her kids whining in the
doorway. For a while our Saturday mornings were a
penance.
There followed, for me, a vivid year of modern
dance. Only imagine the heroics of it: a tiny Jewish girl

in her twenties, tense as a young bird, dedicated to Art,
operating out of a storefront behind venetian blinds. A
few potted plants, photos of Isadora, Ted Shawn and
Ruth St. Denis piously tacked on the walls. Through
her gauze drapery Miss Weinstein was all bone and
dancer's muscle. Her body was covered for Bridgeport,
though sometimes when the mothers had gone off —
they were not allowed to attend class with their clumpy
purses and absurdly disguised shapes — sometimes,
our teacher would fling off her kimono and reveal herself to us, free and naked under her Grecian dress,
leaping, swaying around the shop for her small audience. We felt the walls thrust out beyond the dry
cleaners next door. The stamped tin ceiling arched
heavenward into the insurance office above. Here was
perfect space; and the phonograph playing away. Her
breasts were like small muscles, too. Her buttocks and
stomach flat. We were to believe the human body was
beautiful: Miss Weinstein made it so, her neck tendons
stretched to the sublime. The idea was alien to me.
My arms and legs and all the mysteries between were
called a temple of the Holy Ghost. All the nuns' warn-
ings — never to see, never to touch. One sad warped
Sister of Saint Joseph took the girls aside each spring
and near to hysteria instructed us in ingenious arrangements of lace handkerchiefs into rosettes that, pinned
with a miraculous medal on our more revealing cotton
dresses, would distract the eye from our childish bo-
soms — our very bodies being instruments of the
devil. For the school play we had undressed with large
white towels held in our teeth, covering our shame.
Then came the modern dance. Ruby Weinstein was ridiculous in her abandon, but the ten preadolescent

girls in her class never snickered. Nipples and navels were reasonable in the atmosphere she created. I'd never seen pubic hair, but it was quite the right thing on Miss Weinstein as she danced for us.

In our home-sewn togas we expressed ourselves, leaping (as though against the wind), swaying (branches in spring), falling (in death to the cold floor). There was no technique at all, save the perfect imitation of our teacher. There was no critique, no one student singled out for grace or elevation of style. The only choreographed piece, which we danced finally and disastrously for our mothers, was performed to the "Narcissus Song." We rushed from the corners of the store to a round 1930's mirror set on the floor, fell in love with our respective images, tossed our heads, sighed, leapt, swayed, fell to the contemplation of our beauty again and expired, all ten of us, by the side of the reflecting pool.

At home I played my own record of "Narcissus" when "they" were out. I dashed from the sun parlor to the center of the living room carpet timing each move, the coy little testing of the water with my toe, the flirtatious smile. There was no mirror needed. The true narcissism of adolescence lay a few years ahead: the self-enchantment of my dancing was enough. Imagined away the plumpness and pigtails. Turned to dust my colorless school clothes. Fantasies in an empty house. It was the beginning of my long career as an escape artist. Secrecy was important. No one on the block, no one at Saint Patrick's School should know that I studied the modern dance. I was the only Christian in Miss Weinstein's class, and though the girls were friendly I was content to go off alone in the car

with my mother. I did not want art confused with real
life. The dread ballet classes of former years had been
an ordeal — all the little daughters of doctors and den-
tists, *socialites* from Fairfield in squirrel coats and
Tyrolean skirts, the heiress of a girdle empire escorted
by a black maid.

No, what Ruby Weinstein offered was pure. Art.
Freedom. I had come to know in my childish way
these grand abstractions. Grace and Beauty. All written
on the blossoming soul with an indiscriminate use of
capital letters. Such inflation seems horrifying to me
now. I have no clear idea what freedom is and grace
belongs to children, to one perfect stroke, or to the
talented who put in a lifetime of hard work. So I leapt
out of Ruby's corner with my illusions on the afternoon of our spring recital to adore myself, pink toga
and pigtails, but I was Narcissus no more. They
laughed. The mothers, squeezed back against the shop
window in a line of folding chairs, swapped smiles and
laughed, not cruelly but with a sweet indulgence. We
were little girls again, consigned to another clumsy step
in our advance toward the womanly state. Someday we
would have purses and hats, hateful permanent waves
and face powder soiling the collars of our print dresses.
We would sit in a row like vegetable women, amused
by art, wondering if there was enough in the house for
supper. End of the record. I died by the side of the
pool.

Polite applause, the scraping of chairs and then Miss
Weinstein sprang forth wearing underclothes beneath
her gauze, decent this day. To urgent unknown music
she danced for them, danced against them. Her strong
small body became a force: the sequence of leaps, back

falls, contractions, spun from her endlessly, like magic
scarves. The little studio was charged with her convic-
tion. She was not afraid to expose herself: this was her
Art. She danced till the end of the old seventy-eight
and danced beyond to silence. Yes, her performance
had a manic energy, was routine artsy, but Ruby's
dedication was the real thing. Stunned by such beauty
I went straight to my dreams again, while the mothers,
bewildered but with full respect, clapped and clapped.
There was a sudden intimacy in the storefront studio — "It's meant so much." "Next year, Miss Weinstein," they said, "in the fall." We stood by the jars of
lilacs she had placed on the window shelf for our final
meeting. There was no next year. Ruby Weinstein was
passing through Bridgeport.

In the car my mother called me by a pet name.
"You were very good, Mimi." That was untrue. She
had laughed with the rest. There was no comfort in the
old name. I remember this moment and others like it
when she would draw away as though the years to
come were accomplished and she had lost control of
me. "How will it turn out for you?" she seemed to say.
Then in a soothing voice she went back, back further
to the nursery rhyme that was always mine — "Reeny-
Pen-Pone/ Lived all alone." I was her strange, fat
child, wounded, clutching my toga in a brown paper
bag. She had done her best.

The Attitudes

GEORGE BEGAN to stutter: "B-b-bread, p-please,"
and "P-pass, the b-b-butter." My brother was such a

bright articulate boy any dodo would have known that
the sudden blubbering plosives were a cry for attention.
He must have been nine or ten years old. Though I
was eighteen months younger I knew the game he
played. He would keep it up — the b-bread, the b-but-
ter and the p-p-potatoes — until my mother's anxious
solicitations drove my father to curse George out:
"Christ Almighty, can't you talk? What the hell is
this?" He would ask the question but my father never
cared for an answer other than his own: George was
ruining dinner, making a fool of himself. How many
times had we heard that one of the supreme skills in
life was being able to speak out clearly, even
eloquently, to address the world grandly, as my father
addressed the Kiwanis and Rotary clubs, as the lawyers
(those much-admired rich and clever men) argued
their cases down at the courthouse? And here was his
son blithering out of the b-blue. Today any half-wit
child psychologist could tell us that a little boy with all
A's and "Annoys others. A great distraction!" written in
the nun's precise hand on the back of his report card
was b-bored out of his mind.

It was a crisis and though I hated every meal I was in
awe of George's persistence. At the table he could keep
the stutter going like a twitch, then wash it right out of
his mouth when he played with Mark Gilday and Dick
Ferucci.

"Speak slowly," my mother said, always in there trying. "Think of each word, George." But soon Jesus
would be invoked again and the plates would dance at
our places as my father struck a blow at weakness and
irregularity. Since they didn't want to know all about
us (Freud had not filtered down to our self-reliant

American family), the burden was on my mother, as usual, to make things right. She found a Mrs. Holton: George was to go for speech lessons, though my mother let us know at once that this lady's abilities were not geared to anything so mundane as curing a boy's bumbling conversation.

In one morning she had discovered the finest woman in Bridgeport, too fine for us she implied somewhat crossly. Oh, her children were already ruined, she knew, by the coarseness of our neighborhood. A rough, dirty blanket covered the whole North End. There was no one with any more idea in his head than running up to the Rialto for a double feature. How she hoped that if Mrs. Holton could take George in hand . . . He lasted two lessons, the only boy, made a sissy, waiting for one little girl to come out of her parlor and another one there to giggle at him when he was through. It was easier to abandon the stutter, so I was slipped into his place as an afterthought. Like his melton coat and school shoes passed down to me, I came by my brother's elocution lessons secondhand. My mother must have been pleased that at least one child of hers would be exposed to the art and manner of Mrs. Holton.

Today I can't read a poem out loud that my family doesn't ridicule me. They groan and titter. They intone a line after me with false resonance. No one ever, ever reads like that, they say, deep from the chest like a Barrymore. They claim it's not *me*. La-dee-dah they make my reading sound and I'll be damned if it is — for it's perfectly natural. It *is* me — the tone held up at the end of a line, the elisions and glides, the glottal softening, the hitch of caesura in my voice. Funny,

of course, if you've heard nothing but the flat crackle
of television voices, thin as cheap beer, clinging to the
microphone for dear life. Hurt and proud, I draw into
my memories. A posture I hate at all other times seems
justified: how can my daughter know, poor impover-
ished child with her crush on the golden movie idol of
the moment — he of the starched mouth and droning
masculinity? How can my common-sensical husband
understand, a midwestern kid, the twang of his Saint
Louis relatives in his ears? How can either of them
hear the fine points of my elocution voice, trained
weekly by Mrs. Holton?

It must have been the heyday of the Emerson
School of Speech and Dramatic Art when Louise Holton was a student in the nineties. The photographs on
her dining room sideboard were discreet: a stately
brunet in the full-length portrait carried her head high
with billowing pompadour, pearl choker on a long
arched throat, pretty arms, a rose in hand. White muslin draped gracefully to the floor from the lacy exaggerated bosom of the day. Simplicity itself. The toe of one
satin slipper indicated a positive stance. Nothing so
transient as a smile on her face, the young lady gazed
steadily ahead with an ethereal softness, capturing in
her look some old idea of beauty. There was spiritual-
ity and competence at once in the gentle angle of the
head. The world that this studio photo of young Mrs.
Holton suggested was so far removed from mine that I
never believed in it. It was dream stuff, like the drawings of beautiful ladies I found on the old sheet music
in the seat of my grandmother's piano bench — "The
Last Rose of Summer," "Come Down, Come Down

My Evenin' Star." Another photograph featured a
group of girls all costumed for a theatrical romp —
Shakespeare I presumed even then — and my Mrs.
Holton with arms akimbo, bold as you please in tights,
had placed one foot jauntily up on a tree stump. They
looked a deadly bunch, faking the hearty fun of it all,
their performance captured in mud tones forever. Behind the bric-a-brac of silver plate there was one more
half-hidden photo, not quite admitted to the everyday
world, of a girl about my age with golden pipe curls
and a wreath of roses on her head for some artistic
event. This was the Holtons' dead daughter, Ruth, I'm
sure of that, but God knows in the gentility of that dining room how I ever learned it outright. I was fascinated by the glint of her perfect teeth, the crisp ring-
lets of hair at her temples . . . a child my age, dead.
This sweet and satisfactory girl was infinitely more de-
serving of life than me — that's how I thought of
her — and I stared at her photo hard and long the few
times Mrs. Holton left the room.

That lifeless house where I presented myself each
week after school — the whole somber feel and smell
of it is with me still, the details more readily available
than the arrangements of houses I have recently lived
in . . . the hall with the hideous umbrella vase, art
pottery of 1910, the brown scrub-brush mat to wipe my
feet on, the toppledy coatrack that held its arms out in-
vitingly and then slipped my coats and sweaters to the
floor. A high table at the dining room window held
waxy houseplants that seemed never to grow or bloom
over the years. The scent of brown laundry soap rose
from the freshly ironed cloth on the dining room table
where we began my lesson. Everything in place and

clean, no excess of matchbooks or rubble of dusty pennies from coat pockets, no tattered magazines, not
even last night's *Post* folded out of the way. Nothing
had happened here or ever would. Mrs. Holton's
pupils came and went in a hush. *Mr.* Holton, on the
early factory shift, came home from work, stole in the
door and creaked up the back stairway. I encountered
him once in the upper hall when I needed to go to the
toilet so urgently that I finally asked permission to tip-
toe up to the immaculate bathroom. There he stood, a
lean Yankee the color of tallow soap. He wore his factory identification tag on the pocket of his blue work-
shirt and black lace-up boots. He did not speak.

Herbert Holton was a foreman at Jenkins Valve, an
engineer in better days who had come down from Massachusetts to get work. Of course Louise Holton was
not from *Bridgeport*, that, my mother pointed out, was
easy to tell. Though she was loyal to our "Park City"
my mother had some fix on Boston that we got a dose
of now and then — the finesse, the delicacy of Bos-
tonians made us all look like boors. Even the Boston
Irish (she was so ignorant of the world) were better than
the breed at home. So off I went to Mrs. Holton, who
was Boston and culture, that I might acquire the clear
rich speech and poise of a lady. Herbert came home.
The stairs creaked. My teacher's voice rang through
her modest house with the assurance of a grande
dame, "Good afternoon, Herbert!" The brightness of
her greeting was always met with silence, and brighter
still she turned back to our lesson.

A, E, I, O, U. We slid the vowels up, then down.
We trilled them and shot them like spitballs at the
walls, in unison, then on my own. I advanced to the

more difficult roller-coaster effects, A, E, I, O, U —
taking each vowel in death-defying swoops. Next, we
addressed ourselves to those troublesome consonants,
the D's and T's, spraying them lightly across the table,
moving on to the plosives, those B's and P's George
had picked to taunt us. All warmed up we let the vo-
cal cords rest, closed our exercise books and went
through the open arch to the living room. There we
faced each other across the carpet — Mrs. Holton, a
corseted full figure in her dark afternoon dress, her
fluffy white hair pinned up in a modified pompadour,
powdery white arms and neck, high color in her cheeks
that even a child would not mistake for rouge. I was
short for my age with plump legs encased in the brown
lisle stockings prescribed for all pure Catholic girls. My
usual school dress was a muted plaid to minimize my
round tummy and each morning my mother finished
me off with glossy fat braids. We swung our arms up
and around. We bent from the middle (neither teacher
nor student had a discernible waist) and lolled our
heads round and round to loosen up before we began
The Attitudes.

When I was first out of college, learning to hold my
liquor and trying to enchant the world, I used to *do*
The Attitudes at parties. Most anyone could sing old
songs, but my skill in pantomime was acknowledged as
special and antic, though my pick-up audiences,
like my family, never believed in me. I like to think I
am the only living person who can perform this lost art
form. All the gestures of life boiled down, jelled to a
routine and practiced first to the right side of Mrs. Holton's living room, then to the left: Calling (hand
cupped to the mouth), Looking (hand over the eyes),

Hearing, Greeting, Farewell, then into the deeper
emotional material: Rejection, Fear, Love (both open
and guarded variety), Laughter (head tossed, eyes dancing) and my favorite, Sorrow. Sorrow was posed with
the head sagged, eyes covered with one drooping arm
while the other was thrust back in limp Despair.

Week after week I mirrored the example of Louise
Holton's perfect Attitudes. I could imagine her Calling
Herbert to come downstairs after her pupils had departed, giving him a Farewell at the front door each
morning as he went off to work with his black lunch
pail, and naturally the most touching of all scenes, I
envisioned her balanced in Sorrow over the photo of
her dead daughter just my age. For what else could be
intended but an elegant mime of life: I was to get my
emotions fixed, to harness my awkward moments into
ideal gestures and thus would my feelings be elevated
to the ideal realm.

At home, to irritate us all, my father sat down to
dinner in his undershirt, actually the top of his BVD's.
My mother might say, "Put a shirt on, Bill," but could
not pursue the matter. He was perverse and crude, a
man who must have his way. I was humiliated by the
scene between them: his childishness — demanding
ketchup and ice water, finding fault with the butter
fresh from the dairy that day, thrusting his freckled
hairy chest out defiantly. Her painful submission to
him brought a short uneasy peace. Then he was an-
grier than ever and provoked a fight with me or George
for not helping our mother. Couldn't we see how
dragged out she was, all afternoon cooking the pot
roast, baking apple pie? How many families did we
think were waited on hand and foot by a blessed mar-

tyr? How many of our friends, poor kids that they were
in two-family houses down the street, were eating her
homemade chocolate cake? You bet your life they're
eating crap off Louie's shelf your mother wouldn't feed
to the dog. And weren't we chauffeured to our lessons — clarinet, elocution and dance? For what? For
us to sit at the table and be distressed — oh, it was too
bad — by his undershirt? Once lathered up he could
go on with great disdain about "educated" people.

George and I were miserable, choking down the
chocolate cake or custard, whatever gift had been given
us that day by our sainted mother — there was no easy
Attitude to take. I had only the beginning of a notion
when I was in grammar school of my father's delight in
his own rhetoric. The next night he'd strike quite another pose — fully clothed, indeed, sporting a well-
tailored suit from Fenn–Feinstein in New Haven —
we'd all be taken through some intricate legal proposi-
tion that had come up at lunch in the Stratfield Hotel,
or, the Latin and Greek roots of our common English
words would be expounded and he would have a
"sliver, darling — ah, that's not a sliver now" of our
dessert. Charming and urbane, he was the most interesting father in the world and we were his radiant
family. We sat late at the table and played with our
crumbs. My mother's demure laugh pleased me,
though of course it was not Laughter or Joy in the
nobler sense as I well knew. Our passions at home
were too muddled to ever be cast in the classical mode.

The tension between my father and mother must
often have come to a head at suppertime: the
mortgage, the kids, the inner knowledge that they were
both meant for better things. And the other nights —

mood of our family meals was as sparkling
_ne out of a Depression comedy.

, Bill!" our mother said, time and again. "Oh,
_ul!" A perpetual girl, she was never dismayed for an
instant by one of his wild stories. Her role of the innocent must be displayed like a talisman for good luck.
The pact that my parents had drawn up between them
had so many clauses — that he should bully her, cap-
tivate her, honor her: that she should suffer his folly
and respect him: all his windy force against her steady
will and self-effacement.

It was the psychiatrist's inevitable suggestion to me
so many years later that my father was the dominant
figure.

"Oh, no," I said.

"Your mother, then?"

"There is no answer to that question."

And I still cannot find my way through their intricate contract. My Looking and Listening at the dinner table were deeply troubling, yet they were easy exercises compared to the more heroic material I watched
my parents enact — my father's raised fist of Anger or
the white muslin folds and fading roses of what I once
believed to be my mother's Unrequited Love.

The gliding vowels and The Attitudes were most
probably an adaptation of the old Delsarte Method,
techniques not so much for the stage as for the dead
form of *tableau vivant* and the recitations expected of
young ladies. The notion was farfetched, that I would
ever nestle into the curve of a grand piano at some
church social or stand in a drawing room flanked by
potted palms, clear my throat, take the position of

Welcome, left then right, balanced just slightly over
the ball of the foot. In the phantom world evoked by
Mrs. Holton I did recite. There in her parlor I acted
out the poems and monologues memorized during the
week with fitting gestures, speaking from the diaphragm
so that I might be heard in the last ghostly row of her
imagined auditorium. I've lost track of all the sentimental verses that were once in my head, but some of
the frisky pieces, thought appropriate for a girl my age,
remain. One began: "I went to the dentist along with
Aunt Nell," and reached its height of hilarity under
the drill. Another featured "takeoffs" on a row of gul-
lible hicks watching a cowboy movie. I was in great
demand. I never attained the Brahmin ballroom for
my stage but appeared often on the wood platform of
Saint Patrick's School built one step up from the cement floor where big spiders and bubble-gum wrappers
clogged the drains. I recited beautifully whenever
Monsignor Lynch came to visit, when the diocesan
supervisor came down from Hartford to inspect our
classes (perfect classes, presumably, since no changes
were ever deemed necessary). When the parents came
once a year, dressed in Sunday clothes, I recited an
elevating poem and did the darling piece about the
dentist as an encore. Dick Ferucci gave them "Ave
Maria" on his violin. Mary Morton, a giddy girl, fumbled over the piano keys: "The Barcarolle," "Country
Gardens." A few flashy types, new in the neighborhood with the defense plants' hiring, tap-danced
and did acrobatic splits. We all sang "To Jesus' heart
all burning/ With fervent love for men."

I recited at birthday parties and when company
came at Christmas and Easter. "Cute" I must have

been up to a certain age, insufferable. Then Mrs. Holton delved into her file cabinet and brought out yellowed sheets of paper — the great readings of English
poetry and prose, all of our literature clipped and
pasted up for the genteel recital. I was Puck, Richard
II, Portia, Lear, Mr. Pickwick, the Ghost of Christmas
Past, Sir Philip Sidney, Tennyson, Matthew Arnold
and, as they say, many, many more. These selections
were not memorized but read off the yellowed sheets,
the lines preserved in the small blurred print of an ancient typewriter. My final elocutionary triumph came
in the eighth grade. I was given a dramatic monologue
which I was led to understand only an individual of
great talent and sensitivity could deliver. By this time I
knew that in some spooky way the work Mrs. Holton
entrusted to me could only have been performed by
Ruth, gone from us forever with her fresh rose wreath
and sickly smile. This last recitation was of the moment — the words of a British mother saying goodbye
to her children as they were about to sail off to the
safety of America during the war, while she stayed
behind courageously, bombs soaring overhead. "Chin
up, Gerald. That's Mummy's boy. It's going to be such
fun, the tall buildings . . . and the Statue of Liberty
will be there in the harbor with her torch of freedom to
welcome you. Pam, my little one, what's this . . . not
tears?" Farewell (to the right), Bravery (center), Sorrow
(left).

I moved myself to choking sobs in rehearsal. The
nuns were thrilled. I don't feel shame now but wonder,
as though it were not me at all but some other self with
a preadolescent idea of the tragic, a puppet girl bab-
bling a text that must have been clipped out of a church

newsletter or a women's magazine. A friend of mine, now a distinguished guardsman of our culture, was made to recite the Gettysburg Address when he was a boy before the entire city of Gloucester, standing out in a mist in front of the statue of the noble fisherman. Painful, funny, but his act was no more ludicrous than my version of the brave British mum waving her kids off: "It's only for a while, Pam. This frightful mess will soon be over. Write to me, darlings. No, Gerald, we must never say goodbye."

Departure was almost as good as death in this despairing war-torn world. A boy I loved moved out of town to an army base. I mooned about the house and ate . . . "Oh, my darling, be brave." I had pimples coming on and "difficult days" when I should not ride my bike or swim. Without warning there was a miraculous coming of age: I began to see the nonsense of my afternoons with Mrs. Holton and felt that I had been badly used. By this time I went freely into her neat refrigerator to get myself a glass of ice water. There at the kitchen table I saw two places laid for supper. The stage was set to unfold the steady disappointment of their lives: Louise and Herbert face each other over another silent meal.

I was humiliated by my past performances. I forced my mother to make excuses for me: it was understood that with Latin and algebra, field hockey in the afternoons at the convent school I now attended . . . There was a cool friendship of sorts that continued between the ladies, Christmas cards, infrequent phone calls. I was lectured on how lucky I was to have been "exposed" to Mrs. Holton. I saw only the ladylike speech and scrim of empty gestures that was meant to

separate me from the hard realities of life. Each adolescent Love and Fear was different. I threw the Delsarte
Method out as trash: my responses to my father and the
games he played with us each night were unpredictable
and often graceless.

This should have been the end, but a few years
later, when I went to public high school, I was involved in a cheap incident that shocked my parents
(the particulars hidden, fortunately, in some obscure
corner of my mind). In this crisis, as with George's
stutter, my mother treated the disease of my rebellion
as a surface wound. Mrs. Holton was resurrected.
This last effort to save me lasted only a few weeks
before I declared myself one of the damned. Not elocution this time, but etiquette — an orrisroot and al-
mond-water finishing process lay in store for me in the
silent parlor. Herbert was dead and Mrs. Holton lived
on in her perfection. She had assembled, on the clean
cloth of the dining room table, books and pamphlets
from the Emerson School. A lady always carries her
head high. Her beauty is enhanced if the lips be
slightly parted. She sits with care. She may cross her
ankles but never the knees. But all was not superficial
deportment: I was to beware of the double entendre
and its lowly offspring, the smutty story. On these
unforgivable occasions, thrown in with men of little
breeding, et cetera . . . I was to turn my head deci-
sively away or say with stern demeanor, "I do not understand."

I was in love with an Italian boy and we walked the
North End at night, kissing between streetlights. His
three buddies like a Mafia escort trailed half a block
behind. He sang with a big band in the Ritz Ballroom

at Pleasure Beach on Saturday nights but we knew my father would never in a million years let me go to a dance hall. We walked down back streets to a pizza parlor where we sat alone feeling each other under the table while his friends were posted guard in the booth behind.

Good-natured laughter is permitted in the home but is not tolerated on the street or in a public conveyance. I must subdue a gloomy mood before entering society. I must practice walking with a book balanced on my head and, above all, not afflict the world with any dismal account of my circumstances. "It is presumed," Mrs. Holton said, "that each one has trouble enough to bear without being burdened with the sorrows of others."

My boyfriend was diddling with me. He had a girl, a smoldery Italian beauty who took the secretarial course and it was presumed — each one has joy enough — that they would marry. I loved the smell of him and the strange beads of sweat that sat on the flat tip of his Sicilian nose and were brushed against my cheek when we embraced.

When I was in college Mrs. Holton died. Months before, she had called my mother and asked if I might come to visit during spring vacation. So on a chill bright day, the forsythia improving the small front yards of Bridgeport, I drove out to the Fanny Goodwin Home for elderly ladies. Her room had the familiar photos, clean linen doilies on the tables, plants and a hot plate. We drank Nescafé. I said that her elocution lessons had served me well. I was constantly asked to speak at college meetings and I announced the Glee

Club from one end of New England to another, speaking from the diaphragm, sliding my vowels, spitting my D's and T's. She offered me one of two decorative plates as a keepsake. They were both Oriental in style and I felt that I stood in such a false position with her that I grabbed the worthless one, a turn-of-the-century Japanese thing, and left the deep-blue Canton china behind. Then she gave me a grocery carton filled with all the materials of her trade — the monologues, the typewritten selections from literature and the glossy cream-colored programs which memorialized those lofty evening recitals at the Emerson School. She walked down to the car with me past the old girls rocking in the sunshine on the porch and stood on the lawn, head high, lips slightly parted, and affecting me with nothing more troublesome than her Pride and Unguarded Love, she bid me a classic Farewell.

I've often wished that I had that piece about the Second World War, but it's gone. When I divorced, the box was left behind in New Jersey — in a leaky cellar that flooded in a hurricane. I said to hell with it and the family photographs, my Smith yearbook, early manuscripts washed away too: I was getting on with my life. Of least importance was that box of Mrs. Holton's. Good riddance to the bloated eloquence of perfectly enunciated poesy, the techniques of good behavior which had not implemented my salvation. I am not the lady I was meant to be.

When my husband, my ex-husband, came to pick up our daughter for the weekend visit he said: "I'm sorry about the mess in the cellar . . . all your papers."

"It's okay."

We stood in the doorway of my apartment with our little girl's overnight case between us while she shuffled through a shopping bag of her favorite toys. We weren't hardened to our circumstances. We dawdled and laughed a lot. He said he could not braid her hair. Finally they started on their way, but turned to look back up the flight of stairs. I stood above them on the landing, posturing, hand to heart. "Chin up. That's Mummy's darling." I laughed and struck the Attitude of Bravery. "It's going to be such fun. We must never say goodbye."

Role Model

I MISTRUST CONFESSIONS. They seem from the vantage point of my Catholic training to suggest an easy road to redemption. Confessions and absolutions in the old religious doses were a staple of my childhood and, like cod-liver oil, were administered to clean out the system. At seven, having reached the age of reason, I was prepared to confess and receive Holy Communion. The first-grade Sister rehearsed the class. Like brainless automatons we were made to recite the set words of a model sinner over and over: "I stole one apple. I answered my father back twice. I lied to my mother. I forgot my prayers." When the real hour was upon us the simple boy in our class, whose head lolled to one side, took his turn in the confessional and announced in a loud uninflected voice: "I stole one apple. I answered my father back twice. I lied to my mother. I forgot my prayers." We were shocked. Our teacher flapped across the aisle and pulled him out from the darkened booth where he defiled the sacrament. Poor dope. If God couldn't forgive him his witless transgressions, how could He hear my intentional and real sins.

And I was a sinner from the start, never one of the good girls the nuns fussed over. My soul was always in question and to launch my spiritual life I mucked up my First Holy Communion. I broke my fast, but I didn't have the guts to go through with the ceremony. I could not take the body and blood of Christ into my mouth now fouled by orange juice.

The scene that morning in our kitchen is full of clues, and like the famous marriage contract of Van Eyck, can be taken as a portrait of our particular bourgeois style. White napkins, polished silver, a florist's box, a glass of pulpy fresh orange juice all denoting an event. Indeed, it would have to be a holiday, for one of my mother's precepts in the thirties was that only the rich indulged in orange juice. When we drank it at all it was by the thimbleful and here was a whole glass of pure gold squeezed, no doubt, for my father or brother on this special day. Alone in the kitchen, greedy, forgetting my spiritual obligation, I drank it down and immediately my crime was apparent. My white dotted-swiss dress hung up over the ironing board. My lace mantilla lay gently folded in a puff of tissue paper: it was finer than the veils the parish girls would wear (always, always finer, the single tedious note of our supposed distinction). My white gloves buttoned at the wrists with pearls. These clothes would never be worn. I picked up a grapefruit knife and tried to commit suicide. With a good deal of wailing I sawed at my wrists until they looked as though I

had been clawed by a mean tabby cat, then plunged
the harmless curved blade at my breast. Why, given
the orange juice, was the grapefruit knife there at all?
Grapefruit with a maraschino cherry—that was for
later, for a Communion breakfast. After church
Grandma Burns, Aunt Margaret from next door, my
dashing Aunt Helen and Grandma Kearns, the *very*
Catholic cousins of my mother who hovered nervously
over our religious life—all would assemble in our dining room with presents for me, a little gold medal,
crystal rosary beads, a white prayerbook. I had spoiled
this day for my family: that seemed as important as my
spiritual disgrace. The grapefruit went back to the refrigerator uncut. My finery fit for a child bride was
packed away. I was not good: that idea was set in my
mind. It was not disfiguring like a purple birthmark:
not-being-good was my general complexion, like the
freckles that stained my arms and legs. Whenever I
felt — or feel now — that I am virtuous, something is
immediately suspect. My religious periods have been
genuine only as dramatic exercises. My Girl Scout
honors (thirty-five badges and a curved bar) were
earned when the tasks and the goodwill of the campfire
were already too simple for me. Too many instances
. . . whenever I am particularly kind, nurse the sick,
give to the poor, I make sure I get the credit, then hate
myself for claiming high marks. After the invasion of
Cambodia in 1969 I rushed to the campus in Santa
Barbara to hold hands in a phalanx against the State
Police who were sent to close down the university: a
good cause but I was sanctimonious, conscious of myself as a moral success. My spiritual self-aggran-
dizement is bad but not yet fatal. There is something

decidedly clownish about my transgressions: they seem
either careless, like the drink of orange juice protesting
the idea that I had reached the age of reason, or so theatrical, like the suicide attempt, that my darkest intentions are rendered venial.

The nuns never tired of the apocryphal tale of Napoleon, that black-hearted man: when asked on Saint
Helena to name the happiest day of his life, he replied:
neither his victory at Austerlitz nor his coronation, but
the day of his First Holy Communion. I received
Communion in disgrace on an ordinary Sunday in
some distant parish, wearing my winter coat and hat,
filing up to the strange altar with children who did not
know my name. I felt, too dramatically, that my soul
was ill-fated. It was going to be uphill all the way.

My first meeting with Clare and Leslie Fine was
charged with that false goodness I could not trust in
myself and my last dealing with that glamorous couple,
many years later, involved me in a shameful lie. I was
still little enough to be cute when we met, hanging
around the hot-dog stand at Fairfield Beach, when Mr.
Fine, a man with a cultivated resemblance to William
Powell in the *Thin Man* movies, asked if he could buy
us kids an ice cream. I alone did not order up my favorite Good Humor but said, politely, that I must get
permission from my mother. Odd how phonies attract:
I was just so very dear and special and Leslie was on
the lookout for picture-book kids with fine manners.
Within a week our family was swept into the make-
believe of their lives.

The circumstances of that meeting are improbable—I remember too much of Fairfield Beach. Long walks at low tide over the wet sandbar with clams sucking through the black silt. The raft grounded on its rusty oil drums. Long Island across the Sound and our unromantic lighthouse easily accessible at the end of a stony reef. I cannot invest Fairfield Beach with more than the pleasure of summer days. We came after lunch, swam, night fell. Like all children we wanted to play forever, dashing through the universe in our terry-cloth beach capes — Flash Gordon and Dale and mad Dr. Zarkov. Drenched with citronella we flew off the boardwalk into the night and hid with the soda bottles and torn bathing shoes under the pavilion, George, a girl named Ethel Powers, and me.

My parents had closed themselves off from the world so successfully to create the safe but stifling refuge of their marriage that George and I had little idea of adult company. One of the great thrills of Fairfield Beach was to watch our mother and father talking and laughing with other parents, a sight we would not see at any other time. Then, every night the grownups dished out the same sorrow to us — it was time to go home. Fold the beach chairs, pack up the pickles and the lemonade jug. In the family locker I changed to a limp summer dress, buckled my dingy white sandals. I licked the sea salt on my lips, my shoulders and wrists. The first mysteries of sex and of my own childish sexuality came about in that dark wooden cubicle. My nakedness close to the voices of strangers. Unfocused lust. If, the few times a year that my mother put on a bathing suit she tucked her stockings and girdle far out of sight, then why did my father choose to display his jockstrap

sprung with the shape of his balls on the most promi-
nent peg? The answer to that one can interest only me
and will interest me forever.

Fairfield Beach—all of it's with me—unedited, the
hometown names and sunburned faces, the jukebox
playing the hits of 1940, the printed notice tacked in
the toilets after the First World War, advising the pa-
trons against immodesty, in particular the scandalous
one-piece bathing costume. There were peepholes in
the showers. Dimes slipped between the planks of the
boardwalk lost forever . . . and so forth. The sandy
patch of grass behind the bathhouses where we parked
our car and the splintery wooden path leading to the
office where our locker key was handed to us by the
proprietor of Restmore, John McGuiness, who managed to be cordial and remote at once like a stylish
maitre d'.

Restmore was not a club, but the number of lockers
at the resort was limited and they were kept from summer to summer by the same families like opera boxes.
In many ways it was a closed world, Bridgeport Irish
mostly, lawyers and doctors with their families, some
businessmen and a flock of unmarried ladies who
taught school. It was comfortable, the closest thing we
knew to an appropriate society. My father was popular
though somewhat raucous. Up on the pavilion, out of
the afternoon sun, my mother kept her dignity intact
reading a magazine or sewing by herself. We swam till
our lips were purple and the skin shriveled on our
fingers. Then one summer the Fines arrived from
Westport, commandeered a locker from John
McGuiness and installed themselves on our little
stretch of beach. Chauffeur-driven, they were set up

for the day by a couple in uniform, their beach umbrella unfurled, their expensive holiday equipment
spread out as though this were Malibu or Cap d'An-
tibes. The servants then departed and left them for
their hours in the sun.

Clare, a handsome woman with hair clipped into
high white wings, lazed in long beach robes and som-
breros straight out of the MGM wardrobe department.
Leslie, delicately built, shaky on his feet, wore berets
and ascots, sandals, bright pongee slacks. There they
sat, marking up the shooting script of her next film
among our thermos bottles of orangeade, our beach
balls — a Hollywood writer plunk in the middle of the
sticky fat-legged babies who belonged to the younger
set.

"Would you be a sweetheart, Les?" Oh, the com-
mand of Clare's honey voice as she assigned Les yet
another task, to tuck in her lap robe, to move the
umbrella, to rub her down with suntan lotion. None of
the adults I knew ever touched in public, much less
kneaded each other's flesh. I can remember him bending over her breasts and thighs like a male nurse,
smoothing on globs of pink cream.

"Clare, darling, will you join me in a dip?" he'd ask
before wobbling off into the tame waves of Long Island
Sound.

"Not now, my love!"

We were all shameless, staring like drool-mouthed
idiots. The chauffeur was a slim Oriental like Charlie
Chan's number one son. Sometimes he came back to
pick them up in a starchy houseboy jacket. I felt that
everyone on the beach must share my scenario: in the
next scene Leslie and Clare in silk pajamas are flopped

in deep white chairs, the chink-a-chink of the cocktail
shaker in the background. Kokymoto serves frosty martinis on a silver tray. My idea of glamour was set by the
Fines: all out of the movies, of course, their style and
my fantasy. I don't believe the dreams we embrace so
easily from the silver screen form us unless there is
some touch of reality — with their stage voices and
Noel Coward epigrams, the Fines *did* enter our worn
middle-class setting of the late Depression years. They
came to Restmore every sunny day when Clare was on
the East Coast, for the simple reason that Les loved salt
water and she hated the rocky beach in Westport.
Since they were aliens among us they could maintain
their privacy and we did offer a decent plot of sand.

Then Les, thinking all the children too adorably
"dead-end kids," bought us ice cream. I pulled my
goodness, my splendid little-girl audition (I'd been in
training for years) and got the role. They had a niece
coming to visit them from New York and they needed
a playmate . . . I was swept into their limousine and
off to their wooded estate with running brook in Westport. Shirley Temple enters millionaire's manse. Every
inch of it was perfect, better than the movies, shot in
muted pastels with lots of Oriental tables and jade
statues . . . the ebony concert grand, set to the side of
French doors which led to the garden, was a mass of
photos in sleek silver frames, Clare on the set with
Sam Goldwyn and Louis B. Mayer, Joan Crawford,
Myrna Loy. Leslie had turned his hand to playwriting
back in the old days when the season supported another comedy on Broadway every night and there he
was in a tux with the cast of *Nothing Personal*.

Unlike the movies, the scene in their house (named

"Bravo" on the entrance gate, their license plate, and a lot of swanky stationery) didn't go away after one afternoon. I was transported to Westport often, flinging out scraps of egalitarian conversation to the driver from the deep plush wonderland of the back seat. Like Pip in *Great Expectations* I played with the niece. She was not a beautiful and haughty creature — in fact, she was the Fines's major disappointment, their only heir, a common child from Queens who could not be made fashionable (good for her!). But at the time I more than sympathized with their pain: Phyllis was not possible and I was. They were amazed at my manners, at my interest in all things theatrical, and delighted by my literary wares (a title here, a line there) that I trotted out for our pretentious game while Phyllis cared for nothing but comic books and wads of bubble gum.

We ate in the dining room where the houseboy padded softly over the sculptured Chinese carpet. Clare rang the bell for Leslie's pills. Presented in little silver boxes, the pink, brown, green, chalky white pills were to maintain every limb and organ of that frail old dandy's body which was quickly giving out on him. They had no way with children. Phyllis and I were a captive audience listening to the particulars of their minor surgery and their tales of who signed what contract with whom and which of Clare's serials was coming out first — the *Saturday Evening Post* mystery or the *Companion* romance.

"The *Post* runs in August, darling." It was Clare who sat at the head of the table.

"October, precious."

He contradicted her. But she was always right. Clare was the one who made the money, the real writer. Les, having failed at art, had lived out his years as a minor public relations executive — an embarrassing detail of their lives. She drummed the dining table, a chunky emerald flashing, imperious in her man-tailored country costume and gave Les the word: "*I* signed the contract. You'll be a hopeless fool tonight if you drink any more coffee."

"The *Post* doesn't start until October," he repeated weakly. "One less martini might clear your head."

They argued constantly, bitched each other about the servants, the car, the steak, the collie dog, the authenticity and the dates of the Chinese porcelains. I had never heard adults argue like this. At home on summer nights I could hear the raised voices of the alcoholic couple next door, objects thrown, once even the thud of a body falling. I had a friend whose short-term stepfather hit her mother often and gave her a clout for good measure. In my innocence I felt that the Fines's verbal swipes were light and easy to take. Now I know that it was rotten: their laughs were the chill gagging of Strindberg. This flamboyant successful woman needed her little man and she needed to destroy him. The bickering was Leslie's way of further demeaning himself. Soon it was "darling" again, "dear heart," mutual "precious love," with more endearments than are called for in the usual marital script.

When the Fines went out, Phyllis, in a proprietary manner, took me into their separate bedrooms and baths. She opened drawers to display Clare's satin underwear and kid gloves. The inconspicuous oil painting of Italian cows swung up to reveal, Hollywood style, a safe in the wall. His dressing room was more dazzling than hers with jackets for every occasion and mood, shirts stacked in a special cupboard — some were silk like Jay Gatsby's but others were woven of coarse linen in tablecloth checks and flowery prints I could not then imagine on a man. There was an excess of cashmere and leather and cologne in this glorified closet. I thought of the strained calculations, right down to the last dollar, that preceded my father's trip to New Haven to buy a new suit and of my mother sitting out in the sun parlor where the light was good, ripping off worn collars and cuffs, reversing them by hand to extend the life of a shirt. The Gatsby reference came later, of course; but my true feelings of awe and stifled resentment at "Bravo" must stem from these cramped comparisons to my Bridgeport life.

Phyllis was a dark sexy little girl who wore red nail polish and charm bracelets. She goaded me into trying on Clare's hats and shoes which she held in great contempt. Oh, how she hated the fine clothes they made her wear on her visits to Westport — and she hated Clare and Les, not because they were frauds (neither one of us could discern that) but because she was stuck here in the country with me when she could have been out at Far Rockaway with her own crowd. Phyllis didn't have much use for me but she dragged me along into the woods where luminous clumps of thick white birches grew. There, hidden under a rock, she kept her comics, gum, and a pack of cigarettes. She was a lousy kid but I couldn't give up my weekend visits to the Fines's. Watching what I took to be the ordinary rich at work and play became an addiction. After the initial wonder, amusement set in: the studied elegance of "Bravo" seemed silly even to a child. But I did learn something: here, as though assigned to me in textbook

jargon, was my role model, the woman writer. There
were times when we were all excluded from Clare's
presence.

For years I was stunned by the boldness of her life:
she removed herself from the household to *work*, while
Les, poor dilettantish fop, was left to his own devices.
During the years I knew him, he designed a Buddha
penny bank and a toothbrush for children with a
clown's head at the top. I resented being sent off to the
woods with the boring Phyllis while Clare Fine laid
claim to a lively personal world. She withdrew to a big
leather-topped desk in her dim Englishy study after a
good deal of superior talk about deadlines and commit-
ments. I wrote two novels in the corner of a bedroom
before I realized that my prejudice against writers' dra-
matizing themselves and the tools of their trade went
back to my status of outcast. Why did I loiter on the
damp ground those dreary afternoons, choking on my
first cigarettes and listening to Phyllis's precocious sexual adventures . . . for what? For the sham of the
clicking typewriter churning out trash in Clare's
study — those slick psychological stories of the forties
written to become scripts for the female stars of that
era, dramas that always simplified a neurosis, Warner
Brothers' Freud dished up for a moment of hysteria in
the movie houses. But I've pushed ahead now to a later
position. . . .

At the time the years went by smoothly and it was
always pleasant though odd to know that the Fines had
adopted me and my family for their limited contact
with the Restmore crowd. World War II: Clare and
Leslie Fine lent strong civilian support to the Canine
Corps. Patriots from all over southern Fairfield and

Westchester counties were encouraged by them to con-
tribute their beloved pets to be trained as guards and
brave dog-soldiers. Phyllis cheapened quickly, could
not even be bribed into taking courses that would pre-
pare her for college. I recall my final visit to Westport — more sterling than ever, I curled up by the fire
with Eugene O'Neill's early plays while she leafed
through movie magazines, her lashes gummed with
mascara, her mouth blood-clot red, set in a perpetual
pout. Phyllis had thickened: big bust, broad ankles and
knees. Her short skirt rode up over her thighs. We
waited in the pale Oriental living room for the Fines to
take us to a restaurant on the Kings Highway. The
chauffeur had gone off to the army, so Les drove.
Timidly putting along at twenty miles an hour, he
stopped at every corner, honking, honking at the
empty back roads. We arrived at the center of town
honking like louts after a wedding, the Fines in their
ridiculous country outfits and Phyllis done up like a
tart. That last weekend was painful — the cook-maid
had taken a good job at Bridgeport Brass. Leslie made
breakfast. Every poached egg was a production. At
noon sandwiches took an hour to shape up like the
chorus line of one of his Broadway flops. Three times a
day, year in, year out, my mother got the food on the
table without much fuss, but Clare raved, "Les is adorable in the kitchen. You simply would not believe the
man's genius!" With the very hands that manned the
typewriter, she buttered our toast. We did the dishes, a
drawn-out finicky project, washing all their foreign
pots and ramekins. Their arguments were fierce and
more frequent given the burden of their wartime duties. Clare was at full power then and wrote letters to

the local papers — "charming little papers" she called them — the *Newtown Bee*, the *Westport Crier*, the *Bridgeport Post* and the *Herald*, begging for gas coupons to help transport the volunteer dogs to basic training. In a million ways they irritated me, still I was quiet and good, smart, polite, everything they wanted. My worthless motive must have been to outdistance Phyllis by a length and a half. She played Stan Kenton records with the volume turned high.

It would have ended there, but I'd made the "Bravo" Christmas list and faithfully they sent me a scarf, gloves, a leather diary — all good stuff — and just as faithfully I wrote my thank-you note. Their Christmas cards, printed on heavy cream stock, featured Les's inept sketches of the woods in Westport or a winterscape of their Park Avenue — it had to be Park Avenue — penthouse.

Clare turned to television plays when the industry was young — not-very-baffling mysteries with a clever lawyer as centerpiece and predictable courtroom revelations. To get her details straight she consulted my father, the Detective of Fairfield County. By this time we had moved to my grandfather's big stucco house (the one grand gesture in our family history) and I'm sure it pleased my father no end to have Clare Fine (with Les) solicit his advice in the largesse of our living room in Bridgeport. He did know, better than the lawyers he worked for, the procedures in a murder investigation and how to present state's evidence. I can recall coming home from college to find my parents anxiously awaiting the hour when Clare's "play" would be shown. I only caught this one example of her late work — stilted acting, the camera glued to one spot swiveling from prosecutor to defendant — talk, talk, talk, exposition, character development, psychological motivation — all the bald techniques of cheap fiction. Suspense, like the rickety studio set, was built with crate wood and penny nails. We began to fight during the commercials. "If you're so damn smart, *you* write one," my father said.

"Write what? A murder for morons?"

"You think they pay her all that money because she doesn't know what she's doing?"

The show was probably no worse than endless hours of drivel I've watched and defiantly enjoyed since, but I had just begun to write my undergraduate verses, Spenserian love sonnets and exercises in terza rima, the sterile games of an inexperienced heart, which disclosed the triteness of my schoolgirl passions. I felt the lines between high art and popular culture to be clearly defined and ranted on to my father about the vulgarity of his world that accepted the *Reader's Digest*, the spongy best-sellers of the day, and now Clare's hokey television play. He probably retaliated with his favorite line: "You should have her income," and for certain he struck the lowest blow of all: Clare wore a lavish mink coat when she'd come to check the legal phrasing in her script, and Leslie, honking into our driveway, drove a Cadillac a mile long.

"Clare doesn't know anything in her goddamn mink coat."

"And you do?"

"Yes, I do," I said with bravado, hardly knowing my way beyond the next history test on the Holy Roman Empire.

In my sophomore year of college when I was adver-

tised, somewhat sarcastically, by my parents as a
member of the literati, the Fines sent me a Christmas
book. It was mailed out from Scribner's bookstore and
arrived at my dormitory shortly after Thanksgiving vacation. Phyllis, they wrote on the gift card, was
engaged. That was that. They hoped I would have
"scads of pleasure from this adorable novel" they had
both loved so much. The book was sentimental
whimsy by an author popular in the fifties whose income could easily have covered lavish minks and mile-
long cars. Alone in the dormitory one Saturday night,
filled with a wallflower's self-pity, I actually read their
gift book. I fed myself the pages, gorging on my righ-
teousness. How wretched — the bravery of an eccen-
tric old lady and her scruffy dog in postwar London.
How bathetic —the old girl's skill in uniting the witless
young lovers. Here the tears. There the sighs.

My marks were high that semester. I had swept away
those vacant years with the nuns. Without thinking of
it as a competition, I had outdistanced the girls from
Brearley and Emma Willard and from the famous
American high schools in wealthy suburbs. I would be,
if not popular and thin . . . but it wasn't that either.
After one spectacular semester I lost interest in my
grades. I would live with poems, poring over my
stubby anthology of modern verse. Though I loved
Yeats and Eliot, like every English major of those
years, the metaphysical poets were my sustaining fare;
and criticism, what I thought to be the cool elegance
of the critical mode, was my heady delight. I knew
Eliot's essay on *Ulysses* before I read the book and
Shakespeare's sonnets came to me through William
Empson's discussions of their logical and grammatical

disorders. My nighttime revels were all with older gentlemen, the New Critics. Here was the good life,
surely: I could afford to miss the Smith prom with
some drunken blind date from Dartmouth, for I
danced at my own cotillion with Mr. Ransom and Mr.
Tate.

Weeks went by and I did not write a thank-you note
for the "adorable novel." When my mother asked at
Christmas if I'd received a present from Clare and
Leslie, I lied. I said I had not received their book or
any note about Phyllis getting married. I'm a rotten
liar, yet when they called it was easier to repeat that I'd
never received the package from Scribner's than to
praise the trivia they'd sent. Phyllis was married now,
Clare said. "It was all rather quick, darling." *That*
meant something. She had married a fellow in "her
neighborhood," in her own dumpy neighborhood of
Queens half-houses was implied.

Good for her, I thought. She didn't want their stage
set: the carved jade and bellpulls and monogrammed
matching everything. She didn't want their squabbling
and the terrible strain of holding all that chic together
day after day, morning and night, sweetheart.

With false modesty I confessed to my triumphs at
college — the poetry prize, lead in the sophomore
play. My priggish tone must have gotten across to
Clare: her replacement for the "lost" present waited for
me on the mail shelf of Martha Wilson House when I
got back from vacation. It was a copy of Willa Cather's
On Writing, a tribute to me that I had forced. Com-
pounding my folly I mocked this too — Willa Cather,
that wholesome woman writer the nuns had pushed at
us. "Almost a Catholic," they said. "Very sympathetic

to the Church." *Death Comes for the Archbishop* and *Shadows on the Rock* were presented as the classics of our age. With my nose in the air I leafed through Miss Cather's essays. They seemed piecemeal on the one hand, overly explicit on the other. Her simplicity was repellent to me.

Leslie died. Clare followed soon after. Her obit in the *Times* carried a picture of an unrecognizable young woman with dark shingled hair and steady eyes. I knew her, I said to myself, I knew her in another form and having known Clare Fine at all seemed bizarre at the time, out of context with my married life in a New England academic community where I was writing my New England academic novel. She had turned out so many mysteries, love stories, novels, scripts, plays. Like a true professional, she had gone from task to task for forty years. Her words were never remembered after the houselights went up or the television set clicked off. She had died suddenly in California while on a studio assignment. I had not known, until I read the obituary, that she was a Quaker from Pennsylvania or that her husband, Leslie, had written the Dewey campaign song in 1952. Naively associating their brand of show-biz sophistication with the Democrats, I was surprised to find that we were on opposite sides of the fence politically, yet that seemed fitting, too. I had always felt patronized by the Fines: the poor girl come to play and, learning to deceive, I had played their game. For years I filed them away under "Miscellaneous — Slightly Embarrassing" along with the Luftwaffe pilot, an unregenerate Nazi I drank with on a transatlantic crossing, and my performance, while a

faculty wife, as Antigone. I attributed to them my dis-
like of glamorous types who carry on every time they
boil an egg or grow lettuce, weighting the ordinary
things of life with their own self-importance.

Now, in the past few years, Clare Fine — her story
has come back to me, settled in my mind, fully fur-
nished. Admitting that I was a young prude to reject
her (the self-serving confession I so mistrust) reinstates
the rose and green silk of her bedroom, the spidery
chrysanthemum on her dressing table reflected in the
triple mirror. Yes, all those glass powder pots were
Lalique, I know that now and I know that Les (his
lineup of silk dressing gowns, ascots, velvet mules,
bowed dancing pumps, and espadrilles is there in my
mind to confirm the old suspicion) was not "straight."
Hindsight is common and bland as boiled potatoes.
(But of course, the young insurance agent came so
often to pretty Mrs. Jones's house in the afternoon!)

It is more important to confess that I have read,
reread, and taught Willa Cather—not everything, not
the piously researched later works, sincere, well-crafted
novels in their classy Knopf bindings, but the inspired
stories written when she was aflame with the desire to
write them and when she had the nerve to confront big
issues—the transience of youth and beauty, love relin-
quished for ambition, the bitter triumphs of success—
what the past will yield if we are truthful. Willa Cather
was fascinated by artists, by those who have the energy,
as she did for some years, to work in the name of art.
And she knew that the artist was selfish, a malcontent,
wanting the marriage bed and kitchen smells of life but
belittling them in his imagination. After her best work
was done Willa Cather turned to the study of mys-

ticism, seeking peace in the grandeur of ritual and nature, supporting herself and her career with honesty. "Ideas" about the Spanish Southwest and the French-Canadian frontier "interested" her, came to her from the outside; too bad, but no disgrace. Her criticism is lucid, plain talk in which art is art, commerce is commerce, life is hard. No one today, least of all those who follow the arabesques of literary criticism, pays any mind to Miss Cather's *On Writing*, but Clare Fine read it hot off the press and sent the book to me with a note proclaiming it full of wisdom.

Coda: My brother, amused and amusing, showed up with a present, not ready to hand the package over. "What famous woman author you know, you *knew* . . ." The usual tease, then he unwrapped a faded violet book, once royal purple with title of gold, *Backstage* by Clare Fine, 1923. Seven tales of the theater—the glitter, the romance, the disillusion and, as she points out in prose that matches the book cover, "scenes from the Great White Way of life, the crossroads of laughter and tears, the *Comédie Humaine*." The stories are set off by two febrile essays about "the mystery of make-believe," the art of the drama which "lays magic fingers over tired eyes." We are onstage, playing our parts in "the house of dreams . . . Is it to be alight or dark? Do we live or die? Tomorrow holds the answer."

Backstage is full of what used to be called colorful writing and vivid characters: there are theatrical agents mouthing cigars who say "kiddo," society clubmen who call each other "old man," wicked impresarios, sullied chorus girls, and there is one icy prima donna with "Jap-like eyes." But the stories are strong: they move along with their own melodrama — I read them in one gulp, late into the night. The hometown girl becomes a star. The brilliant actress gives up all for her man and losing her glamour, loses his love. The starving young actor receives his first great ovation as his sweet wife dies in the gringy loneliness of their boardinghouse. There is a sense in this first book that Clare's strongest impulse was to be a writer and as for the tales, she was under no obligation to feel them. She relied on the theatricality of her plots and the sure-fire appeal of her Broadway folk. She certainly knew their world and was making it hers in 1923, but she never gave herself completely to the house of dreams. These many years later, it's her turn to force the tribute from me: she had her career and believed in it: *Backstage* was not a bad beginning and she wrote to her last day.

Often I fear that there are books ahead of me —mysteries, perhaps love stories, the suggested television drama or an "idea" for a book that might interest me. I am terrified of the repeats, the stock responses: I stole one apple. I answered my father back twice. I lied to my mother. *Mea culpa, mea maxima culpa* — there are times when I am so tired of last year's cloth coat, five flights of stairs and the old Volkswagen, I would sign a contract, any contract. In the darkened theater of my make-believe it is only a matter of time before the houselights go up. Then I will sit at my leather-topped desk, ring for the houseboy and my husband to be witnesses as I sign myself away for the fashionable pastiche: I'll wait for something like absolution and all the time repeat the words of my mentor, Miss Cather —

"The courage to go on without compromise does not come to a writer all at once — nor, for that matter, does the ability" — like an enigmatic prayer.

Follow That Car

MY FATHER WAS a terrible man. I know I'll spend too much time in taking that statement back. My efforts will make Bill Kearns out to be a good fellow who easily drove his daughter to distraction and at times to flashes of anger that came close, very close to hatred. If he hadn't been my father I would have loved the spectacle he created — one performance following quickly upon another — like a versatile old vaudevillian with his audience (wife and children) in the palm of his hand. But I am his daughter and it's no mystery that he is the model for the charming, self-dramatizing men I'm drawn to.

If you look at it one way, but we never did, my father was a glorified cop. He was the Detective for Fairfield County all of my childhood and we were duly impressed. He had a courthouse swagger, a fluent tongue and a gentleman's manner that was unlike that of a petty official or civil servant and he knew it. He should have been a lawyer or a judge, a man of some importance, but he had been a spoiled boy who could not sit at a desk, too clever for his own good. Gifted with a sweet tenor voice, he was the star choirboy at Saint Mary's on the East Side before he was ten years old, wearing a black cassock like a priest's under the angelic white smock that his mother washed and starched each week. He sang "Ave Maria" at the Introit and as the parishioners filed up to the Communion rail took the solo of "Panis Angelicus" so purely that heads turned away from the altar up to the shellacked-oak organ loft. On Christmas there were tears during his "Silent Night." His "Danny Boy" was famous. What a starred beginning in the world, though he looks just an ordinary mug in a class picture (1903) with freckles, the devil's kiss of a dimple in his chin, scruffy high shoes and black stockings with one knee out, squatting in the first row of his class with the respectable kids, a bunch of babies compared to the tall goonish boys and girls who seemed to linger on forever in those old grade schools.

Once or twice when she was weary of catering to him my mother let out that he was raised like a prince, his sister and mother waiting on him hand and foot. He never got out of his chair to get himself so much as a glass of water all his life. I feel that his specialness went all the way back to the day he was born William Satolli Kearns, the queer middle name after the first Vatican emissary to visit Bridgeport. It was May Day and touring the new Catholic hospital Alessandro Cardinal Satolli gave my father his blessing straight from Rome. Early in the game the priests had an eye on him and instead of his going to high school they took this talented Irish kid to Saint Thomas Seminary in Hartford. It was an opportunity not to be missed for his father was poor, a mere attendant at the county jail. In the seminary my father studied Latin, Greek, moral philosophy, rhetoric, apologetics — a schoolboy's smattering of the education prescribed for a Christian gentleman in the sixteenth century. He knew no European or American history, no literature, art or science.

French and Italian were thrown into the curriculum at
Saint Thomas for the quick-witted who might be sent
abroad for further study and that came easy: he ab-
sorbed languages. I cannot sing a note. I cannot speak
a foreign language; indeed, I've struggled against the
odds to pass the necessary exams and it has always
angered me that my father just threw his gifts away.

The truth is that he loved roles, did a superb job of
playing the seminarian, the cub reporter, the law student, the businessman, but like many inventive actors
he tired of long runs. He stayed at Saint Thomas four
years so that many of his oldest friends were priests.
One fellow in the class became Bishop of Pittsburgh.
There seemed to be no shame on my father's part that
he did not go through with a life dedicated to Christ.
Surely he was no more worldly than his pal, the white-
haired monsignor, who came to visit every summer in
a limousine, nails buffed, breasted in red moiré on the
hottest days. The story of my father's vocation had
washed away when we were kids: nothing remained but
his feeling of intellectual inferiority. Either he mocked
"the intelligentsia," pulling a prissy milksop face,
crooking his little finger out from a cup as though that
effete gesture summed up what he thought of cultured
types, or he worshipped men of learning as only one
can worship authority who has been trained as a servant in the Catholic Church. He pouted, whined
when we were grown that he was the only one at the
dinner table — the ignoramus, dunce, dullard — who
did not have a Bachelor of Arts degree.

He read no more than four or five books when we
were children and only subscribed to the *Reader's
Digest* when he retired. Then reading became a ner-

vous habit, a tic after the pill-taking, chain-smoking, channel-switching, the restless pacing of the house which broke up the days spent in his cumbersome heart-saver chair. He did read Hemingway when George went to Yale "to see what all the fuss was about."

"This guy can write one hell of a story. If you kids took your heads out of the clouds you could make some money."

There was nothing to it, just discard some of the nonsense the professors sold us. It was hard enough to see his children revere poets and novelists when what he had in mind was a profitable career for them, advertising or the law.

His respect for Hemingway's prose did not alter his abuse of the man. A picture of that modern master in a ladies' magazine showed him suntanned, snowy-bearded, naked on a bed in Cuba, his genitals covered with a small book. "Jesus, will you look at that old man in flagrante. That's very artistic." Artists were whoremasters and drunken louts. He resented the cultural heroes who were pushed at him in the feature articles of *Life* — Frank Lloyd Wright and Picasso — now isn't he a kiss-me-ass with the little string tie, the beret, whatever. This looks worse than it ever sounded. Such talk was part of his double-edged banter and the lines were said in one of his best guises, a barroom Paddy delivering himself of wise and witty observations. Often when his bigoted opinions drove me to tears he won the argument by dropping the pose. "Well now, if you're going to take everything serious," he'd say, "if we can't have a little fun."

My mother abstracted herself. It was a thin line she

walked in her sensible lace-up shoes. We were disre-
spectful talking back to him, but wasn't it dreadful
when he got on one of his tirades — "That ballet you're
taking them to, Mother, will it have those little men
dancing around displaying their private parts?"

"Bill, please —"

"No, I'm just asking what kind of a pansy . . ."

Up in the back bedroom my brother began to construct a private world of brick and board bookcases —
literary journals, early editions of Pound and Auden,
Wyndham Lewis, Fenellosa, Gypsy Rose Lee's novel,
old Coca-Cola signs, and Victor Red Seal Records of
Nellie Melba and Yehudi Menuhin. Vaudeville gems:
Harry Lauder, the Two Black Crows, Fanny Brice.
Term papers, notebooks, his old clarinet sheet music
strewn on the floor with dirty socks. No one entered. It
was a cold back room over the kitchen with an old
dresser still packed with my dead uncle's shirt studs,
celluloid collars, golf tees and photos of his athletic
teams. In some indefinable way the room was not part
of the house. For a family who had prided itself on
quality they'd thrown down an old carpet and purchased a cheap bedroom set. The brown wallpaper was
an afterthought. A sour bachelor smell hung in the air:
it was George's haven. Though I know he suffered in-
tensely from my father's scorn, my brother removed
himself nicely over the years to a back-bedroom world
of his own making, so cluttered and personal that I will
never expect the ordinary standards of housekeeping
from him nor any flabby bourgeois pronouncement on
the arts. He wanders off after supper in my house (as
he did when my father was alive and taunting us),

closes a door and slumps into the mess of his books
and papers, sleeps through the racket of family life.

For my part, I had to be there answering every jibe,
defending Western Civilization against the Tartar
hordes. My fury deprived me of all cleverness. I stum-
bled into my father's most obvious traps. *September
Morn*, a slick asexual painting of a naked woman that
had created a scandal at the turn of the century, was
his constant reference. "Christ, do you know she's got
a picture in her room — *September Morn?*" (Botticelli's *Birth of Venus*). "You can't send that filth
through the mail" (a postcard of a Matisse nude —
September Morn). Goya, Renoir, Titian — all had
produced versions of *September Morn* — and every
time I leapt for the bait. Where I would have been sar-
castic with a friend's ignorance or adroit in a college
seminar, I defended the beauty of the nude body and
the distortions of modern paintings doggedly, beginning each argument at square A. My father played me
along much as he held me in his grip when I was a
little girl: the more I squealed, the tighter the prison of
his embrace. So, even when I was a grown woman, he
would leave me on the edge of hysteria in all our
arguments: though I married and lived as far as I
could spiritually from Bridgeport, he reduced me in a
matter of hours to a wriggling child, pleading to go
free.

It was an exciting game for both of us and came to
an end only after my father had his first heart attack.
Then the slightest battle brought on a clutching and
fumbling, a dramatic hitching at the left side, a call for
water, pills: he had found his last great role. Deprived
of our confrontations we became another bland father

and daughter, visiting. It was sad for both of us. We shelved our feelings and along with them our passionate hold on each other. A loss of interest. We were nice. And there I was again at that round mahogany dining table forced to witness without protest the monstrous show he made out of his illness. This sounds hard, as though I'm paying off old scores now that it's easy. But his life, his life as my father, has come clear to me and plays before me like a movie, rich, absorbing in every detail. I learned more from his cruelty than from my mother's care.

Arriving at the pier in New York, late August 1958, after a year spent in London, my husband and I were rushed through customs with the first-class passengers, the sort of favor my father could still arrange. There he stood on the dock — propped by one of my grandmother's canes, ashen-faced, crumpled at the shoulders and knees, a bitter old man waving us off. We should not bother with him since we did not care. His floppy seersucker suit and panama hat like faded values of the past were perfection for this scene.

"Your father has had a heart attack," my mother said. This was their news. Oh, it was months ago while we were having our good time in Europe.

"You're back," my father said, rationing out his words like a dying man. "Now I hope you'll know to stay home."

A whole year gone in a moment. The sticky business of real life greeted me with open arms. I had been masquerading in Harrods' fish department and the Garrick Club, walking up and down the carpeted steps of a Regency house. Elevenses with the char. The ex-

hilarating route from the tube station at Russell Square
through Bloomsbury to my daily place under the great
dome of the British Museum: my requests honored for
The Gentleman's Magazine of 1869, for a first edition
of Linnaeus. In Oxford Circus the Berliner Ensemble
performed *Mother Courage* with Helene Weigel. On
the fringes of Soho, Greeks were opening the only
French restaurants we could afford. At the Old Vic red
ribbons dripping from the sleeves of a white gown were
an exquisite choice for bloody stumps in Olivier's
Titus Andronicus — I learned that violence should be
accomplished by stylization in art.

My father had come to the pier in New York to an-
nounce that he was a dying man. I wanted to go at
once to the hotel room and watch him put a digitalis
under his tongue, to hear his gasping breath as he lay
stretched out in his suspenders resting conspicuously. I
had stricken him with pain. I had abandoned him to
wander the big house alone with only my mother to
bring him cups of his heavily sugared cream and coffee.

My father lived on for ten years indulging himself in
butter and salt, thick steaks marbled with fat: "I wish
God would call me . . . it's no use living like this."
Smoking a couple of packs of cigarettes a day —
"What the hell, I'm finished." Taking what pills he
fancied. He grew his hair into white fluffs over his
ears, could fake a palsy or a slouch-mouthed stroke. It
was impossible to tell when he was truly in pain
though he slept fitfully day and night through the curse
of his emphysema then rose and dressed more
elegantly than ever in cashmere sweaters and cordovan
shoes and drove out in his new Chrysler with my

mother on endless errands to shopping centers. It could take a week to find a light bulb or talcum powder that pleased him. On their idle journeys restaurants came in and out of favor. They liked the bluefish at the Clam Box in Westport, the turkey dinner at the Hitching Post, smorgasbord night at Yankee Dover. Condemned to die there seemed a million little pleasures to pursue, a particular English toffee, Viyella shirts, that light bulb with a pinkish cast to cut the glare. George and I were tractable at last, listening to his every word as though we still respected him. He was pitifully short of breath, restless, sometimes troubled in his mind, but what a time he had threatening us all. When he finally died I was surprised to read in his obituary notice what I had not known: he was only seventy years old.

The picture of my father during his staged demise is still with me, his white curls growing over his collar, slouched at the table lighting a "last" cigarette, or, in the hospital playing up to the nurses in his final weeks when death was no joke. He was a courthouse dandy to the last, and I shaved him on his deathbed according to his wishes. My mother fled from the room. His hands fluttered up to take the electric razor from me. "Almighty God, you'll take off my nose." I could do nothing right. "Watch out for my cancer," he moaned, a flaky spot he'd been showing off to us for years, and "Give us a smile," he said.

"Well, this isn't a lot of fun. Do you want some shaving lotion?"

Yes, he did and he was looking fine, ready to go into his coma. "Take your mother home," he said. It was

snowing outside and he saw that we'd skid down the
hill from Saint Vincent's.

He died inconveniently the morning after I'd made a
trip back to New Jersey from Bridgeport. I was absolutely dry-eyed and then in the spring I began playing a
Helen Morgan record late at night — "Just plain Bill,
an ordinary guy," and I wept and wept, luxuriating in
the sorrow of my loss.

"Damn him. Wasn't he the worst man?" I've said in
recent years.

Then my daughter who remembers her grandfather
slightly says, "It sounds as though you hated him."

What a stupid idea: I come up with some feeble
proof of my love. He brought home ice cream if he'd
been out late on a case. On cold nights he made pea-
nut brittle that hardened on the back stoop. Once
when I was in college he came to visit me in North-
ampton by himself and bought me an expensive white
blazer with the college insignia. He was composed and
quiet. We drank old-fashioneds in a restaurant and he
was nice like some man I didn't know. Trying to get at
my father's story I was always tampering with the
books. Time and again I reverted to that sadistic portrait of him as a sick old man, or, turned to the easiest
attack of all — he was a horror to me politically, a vile
Republican who supported Joe McCarthy. Then I
claimed to love him.

I may have it right at last, a balancing of the emotional ledger. For twenty years he was Detective of
Fairfield County with a badge in a leather case and
upon occasion a gun strapped to his body. He drove an
inconspicuous state car. It was a nine-to-five job, every
day drab, driving the county roads or going down to

the courthouse with leeway enough to quit early on a summer's day and make him think that he was his own boss. He traveled the railroads on a pass and went away overnight a half-dozen times a year to work with the FBI and then the chief excitement seemed to be whether my mother would have his good shirts ironed in time, whether his brown bathrobe was too worn for a Washington or Buffalo hotel.

It is not the usual middle-class tragedy, that Billy Kearns had a wife and children to support. His ability to imagine himself over and over again, like an actor, was extraordinary. The scope of his life was narrowed to one domestic scene and all his fancies had to be enacted in our first little house. His groans heard from the bathroom were worthy of blind Lear. His whistle coming in from his day's work was as hearty and false as that Irish gaiety that betrayed so many of O'Neill's disenchanted boys gone gray and balding. He was Mr. Micawber at the kitchen table, the Duke of Bilgewater as we drove out to Fairfield Beach. Once during the First World War he had sprung into real romance and gone off to France in puttees with the Forty and Eight. He had a hell of a time but there was no particular glory in his past and the captured Hun helmet with its Kaiser Wilhelm spike was thrown in the cellar with his old crystal sets.

For twenty years we were covered by his state insurance policy. For twenty years he took two weeks' vacation, a man who should have had top-billing. Minnie Pious, the comedienne, was a courthouse pal, a boisterous girl who'd gone from her typewriter in Bridgeport to the Fred Allen show. Johnny, the Philip Morris midget, had been a bellhop down at the Stratfield

Hotel. Shit, my father had made men cry at Saint Mary's for the likes of John McCormack come again. He had the manner down exactly of a distinguished federal court judge — indeed, his first boss, the prosecutor of Fairfield County, was Homer Cummings who became Attorney General and attempted unsuccessfully to pack the Supreme Court for Franklin Roosevelt in 1937. The faithful might have knelt at my father's knee and kissed his ring. He might have blessed children and tapped Christ's body on a chalice rim. He gave up those roles.

For twenty years he was a hard-working state employee serving subpoenas, collecting and presenting evidence in court. I have such a loathing for movies about cops — the dead contrivance of it all, and the modish academic notions that bloat detective stories into art. I can't watch William Holden or Richard Widmark rush to the scene of the crime, cool and handsome; I don't long for the delayed moment when the tough son of a bitch cracks to reveal he is kind. I can indulge myself in a ballroom scene with hoopskirts or the jerry-built glamour of the Old West, but with cops and robbers the illusion never works. For me there is always the obvious sound track of blank shots and screeching tires. The chase is laughable: the blood synthetic.

The crime never unfolds for me without a picture of my father, dapper in his Edward G. Robinson hat, handcuffed to a felon on the front page of the *Bridgeport Post*. We at home knew that his serious grimace was pulled for his pals, the reporters. He played to the crowd. We never entertained a notion that as a detective he scaled walls, climbed perilous scaffoldings.

Overfed and underexercised he couldn't jump off the back stoop. He was not brave. Once a convict terrorized him with a pistol carved out of balsa wood and crayoned black. With this gun stuck in his ribs my father led the man out past the guards to North Avenue where the prisoner enjoyed fifteen minutes of freedom in the bushes. That weightless pistol, like a primitive toy, was thrown in our buffet drawer. It was silly to think of my father with a magnifying glass scraping bits of blood and hair off the end of a murder weapon.

He lay on the couch, a short, round man, collar unbuttoned, chins set free. With each breath his suspenders tugged at his pants. He snored and sputtered in his predinner nap to make us laugh. I am convinced that even in his sleep he created effects for us — dirigible, grumpy gnome. The newspaper, arranged to tickle his nose, fluttered foolishly over his face with every breath.

I sat in a car with him on a quiet street in Stratford (deep lawns, big wooden porches, the trees just leafing out) for hours on end several days in a row, coloring, cutting out dolls. He pushed back his hat and observed the neighborhood traffic: the bakery man delivered: the laundry truck did its rounds. Somewhere on the second floor of a peaceful house was the biggest bookie operation in southern New England. I was a cover — a little girl with braids. I ran up and down the sidewalk of this unfamiliar neighborhood like a child rehearsing for a movie. Where do I bounce my ball? When do I count the cars in the driveway? It was boring for me and at last he took me off to Brock Hall Dairy for ice cream. At Christmas I was trained to go to the door and refuse presents of liquor and cigarettes.

At the curb by the side of the house a group of sinister men in dark coats sat in a funereal black car.

"My father is not at home," I said primly. I dealt with evil so firmly in those days. There was no contradiction in the fact that the front hall closet was stacked high with Dobbs hatboxes, gifts of the best soft felts and expensive panamas from the plant managers in Norwalk and Danbury. After all, Bill Kearns was famous downtown for the hat pushed back with his thumb, a gesture that accompanied the small performance of his smile. I'd seen him in action: circus tickets, the best box at Thanksgiving football games were easily arranged. I cut school and rode with him through Fairfield County. George never went, maybe they fought too often from the very start, but I was a smug Miss Muffet, happy as a pig in shit on our days together. Cops stopped traffic in the center of Stamford for us to cross against the light. His badge passed us into minor league practice at Candlelight Stadium. We sped along the Merritt Parkway right into the scene with the motorcycle siren and the young state trooper who blushed and saluted stiffly: "Sorry, sir." After this encounter we were escorted to our exit weaving around the cars that puttered along at the speed limit. Petty stuff. Like my father I believe that I am scrupulously honest — it's just that I rip up parking tickets and cry out that the world, the big world doesn't understand that the privileges of the old courthouse on Golden Hill Street must be extended to me.

I'm circling back to the problem of Joseph McCarthy. I have refused to understand my father's admiration for that twirp who manipulated two Presidents. I have tried to justify his allegiance on the grounds that my father wanted revenge, along with the Senator from Wisconsin, on a society that had treated the Irish like guttersnipes and cartoon drunks when he was a kid. Holding fast to a grudge, I've kept my memory of his McCarthyism alive too long. He did not fear Communists more than anyone else in the neighborhood who drove cautiously by the Workman's Circle in the thirties. He knew the men down the block — the Lithuanian grocer, the Jewish immigrants who ran shops over in the Madison Avenue ghetto, the Italian labor leader, the Polish refugees who assembled for the lectures in the modest meeting hall on Capital Avenue. He mistrusted their politics no more seriously than their sausages or their garlic-scented clothes. My version that he had a strong-arm-of-the-law, fascist side to him has been exaggerated. I came to political life in the fifties, a naive liberal, soft at the center, delighted with the United Nations and beguiled by any handsome idealist, Stringfellow Barr or Robert Hutchins, who came along. Joe McCarthy was a distasteful man to me, hissing accusations, flapping his spurious documents in the air — "I hold here in my hand . . ." The insane look in his pig-eyes, glint of an adolescent with a dirty secret. Crusading for our national honor and personal liberty, I rushed in against my father. He would simply say: "McCarthy is a master of persuasion, a great courtroom personality."

"Lies," I shouted.

"Don't make a fool of yourself. The man's tactics are brilliant."

Then, I could not believe that he was interested in an aesthetic performance. He loved the sly maneuvers of lawyer Welch during the Army-McCarthy hearings

as much as Joe McCarthy's scummy techniques. Rhetoric was all. He worshipped every word that came from
Senator Everett Dirksen's mouth, fruity vowels and
ripe pauses, down-home wisdom. Monsignor Fulton
Sheen, on the other hand, was a fake. He "fancied"
himself, dressed in full clerical robes for a television
audience, swishing his cape, fingering a cross: the
whole show was too haughty and aristocratic.

There was a balance between phony grandeur and
the common touch that my father strived for: the perfection of an elusive American style which was as
beautiful and amoral to him as the idea of style was to
Oscar Wilde. His sense of life had once been in his
own sense of performance, but our shoes were bought,
the roof over our heads insured. Steadily, too steadily,
he went down to the courthouse. The outrage at his
children was just. What the hell did we think we were
up to — here he stood in full support of McCarthy's
attitudes — turning into namby-pamby intellectuals or
whatever. We would never find a place out there in
the world. We were an affront to the daily sacrifice of
himself. In my dancing and acting, in my brother's
translations, he could only see children who would
never give up our play, and for all his envy I believe
his fear for us was genuine.

Suppose George and I had lived the lives he wished
for us, high on a hill in Easton or in swanky Greens
Farms. George with big cars, a snappy wife and dark-
haired Irish children, and I the helpmate of a clean-cut
local doctor, lawyer or smart broker with Ivy League
credentials. I can almost see my phantom husband,
the easy saunter he affects as he goes down the drive to
tend the roses he has taken on as a hobby. The sleeve

of his golf sweater, I'm ashamed to say, is torn at the elbow. Who's to say I'd be any happier looking out the window of a large suburban living room, collecting Delft or export china, shopping early for Christmas, "keeping up" with my reading. On his birthday I would buy my brother a first edition of Yeats or of *The Pisan Cantos* as an extravagant tribute to what he might have been in a less-real life. Who's to say we'd be any better off? My father — that impossible clown, inflated impresario, barker, snake charmer, P. T. Barnum of our respectable shingle cottage on North Avenue — would he truly have wanted us to settle for one act: I think because I loved him, coarse and unlettered as he pretended to be, that he would have known from experience that our lives do not admit the fictional luxury of alternate endings.

Dining Out

ONE OF MY MOTHER'S cookbooks, stained with ancient batters, stuffed with household hints, is still on my shelf. It is not a good cookbook, I now know, but full of meals to satisfy the ideal American family circa 1935: broiled chops, fresh overcooked vegetables served with a pat of butter, wholesome breads and fruit salads with decorative spirals of mayonnaise. This book was issued by Crisco — 100% pure vegetable shortening — and the Crisco-white cover features intriguing vignettes of a perky maid, a smug man in a dinner jacket contemplating a T-bone steak and two alluring young women poised over teacups. Until I was married

I honestly thought that recipes calling for large amounts of homogenized vegetable shortening constituted three-fourths of every cookbook. But the fried food, cakes and pies were not of interest to me — what I loved about *The Art of Cooking and Serving* when I was a kid, what I love now, is the introductory chapter, which lays forth with unquestioned authority the program for a fine domestic life.

Here the answers were given, much as they were for the spiritual realm in my blue catechism, to all questions that might arise in the kitchen or dining room. There was an ordained breakfast cloth and egg cup for the morning service: embroidered luncheon mats with gay pottery soup bowls were permissible for the informal midday meal, but white linen, fine china and crystal were obligatory for every dinner. All this was shown in grayish photographs. I believed that somewhere the house existed with that set of high-gloss dining room furniture and the correct assortment of vases in which to arrange the floral centerpiece, as necessary on the table as salt and pepper for each meal. In this household none of the plates were chipped. The napkins were a matched set. The top drawer of this polished Queen Anne buffet contained silver in proper rows, not my father's pistols, blackjacks, his body holster and handcuffs, mug shots of small-time gangsters, a cribbage set, Mah-Jongg pieces and a thin silk flag of kelly green — *Erin go bragh*. Order — that's what I envied, even as a child, in the Crisco house. I still want it hopelessly in my life: objects clean, folded, stacked, an emotional prescription for my days.

A moral position is implied by Sarah Field Splint, the author of *The Art of Cooking and Serving*:

The intelligent woman fits her table to her pocketbook and her strength. It is a sign of good taste to do only as much as we can do well, and to leave the extreme expressions of style to those who have money and servants to carry them out.

What more is there to say? And who the hell do I think I am — buying scallops, veal, artichokes, aerating my béarnaise and gazpacho, mincing and dicing beyond my strength. I have abused myself time and again, boning whole chickens and legs of lamb, my nails clotted with raw flesh. I have glazed patés and salmon late into the night. In a sense I have dined out in my own house, hoping to enter a world I can't belong to and that I now hold in contempt.

In the beginning it did not seem to signify that we lived in an infirmary, an old frame building on the corner of the Williams College campus with rotted boards in the front porch, fire extinguishers at every turn of the stairs, rope ladders hung at the windows. It was called Williams Hall Annex but the structure it annexed had long since burned down. These quarters, not fit for sick boys, were now the homes of the young married faculty, each apartment a bizarre arrangement of hospital rooms. The first floor — public waiting rooms and doctors' offices — was most desirable. Above, the small sickrooms and service kitchens rambled in all directions off a dark central hallway swathed in gray linoleum. The Annex narrowed on the top floor where we lived, two apartments sealed off from the hall; it was obvious that this place was for the quarantined in the old days, before measles shots and antibiotics.

Here my married life began. My life apart from my
parents. Life after the two years of marking time with
those college-girl jobs in New York. Girls were made
to marry and marriage was my only serious pursuit.
My education and career were sham intentions, smart
midcentury substitutes for the embroidery work and
social graces of an earlier time. The endless dalliance
of girls' waiting for a man, for the man, was my heritage. I was overdetermined (the jargon is fitting) to love
and to marry, and, more's the pity, I could only respond to clever men, bright men who lived off works of
art — wanting, I suppose, substance that I dared not
have on my own. In memory the sighs of my first ob-
sessive love echo through the Hall of Graduate Studies
at Yale. My bridal picture tells too much: I am absolutely fierce, set in my purpose, impatient with the
bouffant dress and illusion veil, the hateful lace
mitts — all chosen by my parents. I would have been
happier in a flour sack. I will have this thing I want.
My eyes blaze out at the camera, a scornful smile on
my mouth at the very idea of a bridal portrait, and my
hands, twisted to arthritic grace, hold the dead waxy
flowers of a studio bouquet. Even if I must sit so
posed, so falsely arranged, I will have this thing I want.

The two rooms of that first apartment were small but
adequate. My savings book was spent on two broad-
loom carpets and the reupholstering of cast-off furniture from my family's house. A barrel top found in the
cellar became a quaint table — museum prints, cordu-
roy cushions, etc. But the kitchen, all mine, faced the
public stairway out in the hall. Where once the bed-
pans and syringes were stored, large hospital cabinets
now accommodated my dishes and pots. I unpacked

my wedding plates and silver, my pristine double boiler. I screwed cup hooks into the shelves and hung my cups. The trees and cows of the common Wedgwood pattern dangled over the platters and trays still dusty with excelsior. We started to eat pan-fried meat and potatoes off our plates where a shepherd lingered under a lofty willow and in the distance an English castle had fallen into romantic ruins.

The gray linoleum from the hall spread into the kitchen and an adjustable bed tray on wheels, surfaced in the same murky stuff, was abandoned in one corner. Across the hall a midwestern couple lived, both of them tall and blond, who spoke to each other only in Japanese. She, a missionary's daughter: he, a mathematician who'd been with the army of occupation in Japan. Stiff, impossible prudes, they were middle-aged at twenty-five. They disapproved of our late hours. I was exposed to them in my trousseau finery as I stood over the sink early in the morning, or, fumbling with the can opener at night, trying to throw a meal together after we'd emptied the martini pitcher.

"Please?" she would say to me in English, bowing and smiling, this bespectacled Christian girl. "Who has the money? Him or you?"

Perched in my kitchen door: "Please? Who owns the car?"

"Please? The Steuben vase?"

"You are going to prevent babies?"

I have always felt that someplace in my encounters with the Japs, as we then called them, was the beginning of the lie. The baby-blue Plymouth was mine, I replied. We used condoms because I could not be logical about matters of religion and had only recently lost

my faith. There was something too amenable in my
answers, a foreshadowing of the compliant young matron I would become. I wanted to say get out of my
goddamn kitchen. It's not the custom of this country to
ask the price of my silver tray. On Sunday morning
when we lay abed their high-pitched Oriental jabber-
ing was only a few feet from our rumpled sheets
(through the fire door) as they bounded downstairs, off
to the Presbyterian church.

Dining in I served up oversauced dishes, carrying
them in from the hall in a French earthenware pot.
The invited young couples would invite *us* one night
soon for another pot. It cannot be that all we talked
about was our insecurity. The husbands' precarious
jobs were the one sore spot to be worried. Indictments
of the men in power. We had no position, no place in
the world and never stopped to take much pleasure in
our youth. Our beauty and freedom were ignored
while we all yearned for the goods of dissatisfied middle age. I remember defiant faces, angry voices arguing
late into the night, sworn alliances, cries of betrayal,
the long drone of strategies for survival. But I remember no bodies, no sexual presence on any of those
evenings. One pretty wife from Akron broke the code:
she wore low-cut dresses, her big creamy breasts on
display. At the faculty club she pressed into the dark
suits of her dance partners and let her head drop on the
man's shoulder like a girl at a prom.

There lived among us one wife who danced professionally, driving over the Berkshire Hills to her teaching job. She exercised for hours on end in the Annex
hallway. All her clothes were costumes. The ease of

her dancer's walk was a continual surprise. Unlike the rest of us, she could not sit in rooms at dinner parties giving way to the usual, the expected. She could not hear our gossip or eat noodles and, knowing she was a figure of fun, wore her hair in a ponytail well into her thirtieth year. Oh, but she was scandalous sleeping till noon and then driving off through blizzards over the Mohawk Trail with her records of Hindemith and Cage to which her troupe of college girls would dance. No one took her seriously — we couldn't afford to — and off she went to South America and England doing what she cared for, that's what offended. The few times she got into shoes and a respectable dress to attend an official function she sputtered with laughter after one drink, listening to the important people, squinting her eyes with concentration so she would not yawn or make some odd, distracting dancelike thrust with her hips.

She kept something alive in me — the sense that I could make a choice, if not now, one day — a choice to say no to the first course, to the purse with matching shoes, real pearls, salad *after* with cheese — and to *The New Yorker* as bible. No, to keeping in my place, to joining in the adulation for the Paul Klee exhibit and heavy foreign movies and she knew, though I didn't believe it, that I might drop out of the hot competition in the hors d'oeuvres department. No — someday — to drifting through department stores and dinner table talk. I played a cowardly game waiting and watching, polishing silver, ironing napkins. The guests came up the stairs. I honored the convention of the perfectly appointed dining room, though I did not have

one, and the established order of bread and butter
plates: I face you over the flowers: love me for it.

I did what came my way, acted in the student plays,
worked on political campaigns, typed my husband's
thesis with four carbon copies to be corrected at every
slip of the finger. There was no Xerox in the days of
the Annex. I gave my soul to make the pages come out
right. I did anything to please. In the background, like
a strong sweep of dull-blue sky that we could not value
in a painting, there were good people (some the hated
and feared full professors) who were not substantially
harmed by the world outside. And there were evenings, I must force myself to be fair, when the Annex
seemed free of the rotted stench of academic politics,
our soiled bandages and bloody surgical pads, and
friendship was an accomplishment we all excelled at.
The old skirts and sweaters from college wore out up
on the third floor. After parties our cat drank what was
left in the martini glasses until he staggered off to our
bed. I began to push the idea of being young and pretty
before it was too late, toyed with the students, developed a devastating tongue. If I seem harsh it is because
I see myself as a fashionable young woman in a decorous red cocktail dress and a gamin haircut standing
on the shabby porch of Williams Hall Annex ready to
go out: all style and no content.

Dining out. Favored by those in power for our manners and wit, my husband and I were often invited to
dine in real houses. Wine glass over the knife. Berry
spoon and pudding plates — the world of Sarah Field
Splint at last. To be the gayest and most knowing,
what a small portion we asked for. To be indebted,

from the clear soup to the assorted liqueurs, singing for our supper because we did not trust our own lives, our own fare. I said yes to the academic poetry of that time which had grown out of stale criticism and yes to the limp refined productions of Shakespeare that had begun to seep out of our new repertory theaters over the fetid landscape of high culture and yes to the staggering simplifications of all the Abstract Expressionists, because — ever aiming to please I had let myself be told.

The shame of it: I remember a lunch served up in the back bedroom of a second-story faculty flat in Ohio to Northrop Frye, the literary critic, our visiting dignitary at Kenyon College. The clothes closet turned into a china cabinet looked like a clothes closet, but I had the patched Persian rug, the colonial drop-leaf table, my mother-in-law's reglued dining room chairs, the luncheon cloth and the floral centerpiece (a ten-mile ride to the florist). I sat at the head of the table, a veritable Madame de Sévigné of central Ohio, exhausted by my labors. I cannot remember one word the great man said, yet getting up from the table I knew that I would dine out on having had him to lunch. I will not bore you with the menu which I do remember down to the last braised turnip in the grande marmite. I was charming too, always that, and knew what to ask, had "read up on," if not read his book on Blake. Myopic and proper, bending into his soup, he talked as though we had all wanted really to say something. I got the impression of a generous man, so committed to his work that he could not fathom my triviality.

My life was arranged: I wrote now: I had a calm

friendly marriage, but as yet no child. I had cried
when we crossed the George Washington Bridge heading out to the Midwest and I was right. The loneliness
was thick in the clean air — once a day to the post office, the dry run of flirtations with the brightest students, the long wait for the weekend dinner parties
with familiar faces. A colonial existence which seemed
unreal even as I lived it. At the end of the spring semester when the graceful town of Gambier was suddenly lush and sultry after the gloomy winter, an insane
round of parties began — a nightmare of asparagus
and strawberries, trout flown into the Columbus airport from Colorado, new evening dresses ordered from
the big department stores in Cleveland. The fine
wines — smoky graves, full-bodied clarets — too
much of that talk. The last party I remember was announced as an exercise in *de trop*, a studied decadence:
dinner jackets and thick cream dessert, just the smart
set on into the night and it ended in a drunken breaking of furniture, a shallow anglophile historian jumping up and down on the Dux armchairs until his hostess and his wife were in tears. It is pure accident that
every witness to that joyless violence — all of us divorced.

During the day the men taught. The cramped graduate school existence was over and now they had only
to prove themselves each day in the classroom and write
a brilliant book. The pressures were inhuman. To some
of them their profession was still of interest, but many
of these men, gray-templed deans and full professors
now, were too forceful for the gentlemanly world of
the university they had entered. They sounded in their
competitive talk like politicians or oil executives and

they thrilled to power rather than ideas. Tenure, grants, jousting for position, only one or two spires of the tower were built of ivory.

At that time I wrote a mannered academic novel, actually a parody of that genre and so at a further remove from life. If there is any strength there (I will never look back to see) it can only be in what I wanted that book to reflect: a sense of order as I knew it in the late fifties and early sixties with all the forms that I accepted and even enjoyed: that was the enormous joke about life — that our passion must be contained if we were not to be fools.

Dining In

I'VE HAD MY HEAD in this gourmet cookbook for twenty years now. Let's have something plain, steak and potatoes. Paper napkins. No apologies on my part.

I have wanted for so long to sit like this, elbows on the table and say that I don't need candlelight anymore. It will be all right to turn on the news while we eat: there is no thread of appreciation so fine that it will snap in a homely setting. Look, the silverware doesn't match and we will survive. The news repeats itself within the hour like an old fogy. What's happening has been simplified so we can eat without distraction.

Did you find a parking space? How was the Latin test? Your mother called. The Latin test was verbs and a sight translation, something humorous about a servant and master. Horace probably. Your mother is taking a course in Camus and Sartre with a genial group.

I have long wanted (false locution) — I want to sit

here for a while, turn the set off and approach the matter head on. Later, later there will be basketball. You
had not counted on my love of sports, for that being
real, not the made-up idea of some professor getting
with it, some poet off to the fights or shooting the
rapids and then shooting his mouth off.

Today in the market there was a new boy behind the
cheese counter, a gorgeous stud, shirt open to the
waist, his chest smooth as a Donatello. A hard street
kid displayed against the cheeses. He served an old
man with an aluminum walker and no circulation,
gone purple in the hands and face, no circulation,
shrunken into his suit. The boy got out all the low-fat
cheeses and they tasted together.

"Mm, good," the kid said. Faint smile on the old
blue lips. The cheese will keep longer than that old
man.

"I'm not sure I could live out of the city": my line.

And yours: "Nonsense, there are such scenes everywhere, affecting moments."

Not for me anymore. In Santa Barbara there was
one black fairy, only one, in a red knit cap and nail
polish sitting in the sunshine down on State Street. I
couldn't live there now.

They are reading after I've done the dishes, two
silent figures in the lamplight: my daughter struggling
over a Shakespeare history play, pushed by her private
school to dazzling heights of achievement, souring her
forever on Falstaff and Hotspur; frowning, her stepfather prepares *Paradise Lost* for the nth time to teach it:
"Milton is too Christian for me. I can't assume a generous attitude."

There are two jiffybags open on the bookcase with advance copies of novels by women. Letters are included announcing "a real breakthrough" in both cases. One book is mercifully short and opens with suburban wives chatting lightheartedly about birth control and orgasms. They have a lot of romps out of wedlock then settle down. The other novel, thick as a college dictionary, starts with forced vivacity about high school sex and becomes the occasion for set pieces: as I thumb through I see that the husband is, naturally, a stiff prick — the lesbian affair mildly *louche*, the whole enterprise like a girl making it into the Little League.

For dessert there is store cake and coffee ice cream. Telephone calls: My Moroccan friend with a detailed description of her car trip to the Pennsylvania Dutch country. She has bought nineteenth-century black buttoned shoes for her baby. My brother, studying Chinese for his explication of Ezra Pound, has partially mastered the menu at Szechuan East. Nothing should be made of this: the anachronistic is ordinary. Mickey Mouse Mona Lisa Baroque — so what? The Zulu performance of *Macbeth* in a Roman amphitheater in Spoleto during the Gershwin festival. The accumulation is our culture.

What's on? Nothing: the young doctor has fallen in love with the opera singer who has a brain tumor. The detective is investigating a gigolo who preys on attractive widows. How lovely — the rolling lawns of an estate in Devon, nannies, blood sport, a wicker pony cart . . . oh, oh the vicar once a fortnight and lawn tennis. Their dresses sweep down the terraced garden, voile with lace insertions, hats with poppies of pale silk

tinted to reality. And plummy voices. Even the
naughty maid has her lilting replies in control, "Yes,
my Lady" . . . "No, my Lord" . . . exhibiting years
of gray repertory training. We look out through the
colonnade into the park as it was, to the gentleman
vested as he was, the kiss, gentle as it was, the loyal
gardener and great sheep dog as they were forming a
tableau with the baby in button shoes and sailor cap.
All before the First World War if not earlier. It inspires
one to get out the brandy rather than pop a beer can.
Let us drink to the demise of the cavalry.

Bored because she is not yet contaminated by nostalgia my daughter has gone to her room. Her music
plays on her radio while I succumb to the gentleman
in the leather armchair now berating the uncivilized
Huns. His whiskey is tea. His library books are false
backs, matched sets of emptiness, tooled spines of
Plato, Aristotle, Goethe. And I am spineless, ignoring
Emerson, always my announced model:

Our houses are built with foreign taste; our shelves are
garnished with foreign ornaments; our opinions, our tastes,
our faculties, lean and follow the Past and Distant.

Yet here I sit wallowing in my guilt while the villainess
in an enviable riding habit canters across the neighbor-
ing downs.

The cat has torn the couch to shreds. Rain is predicted: the spaghetti pot and a soup kettle are placed at
corners of the rug where the skylight leaks. I had
thought of setting plants underneath but the inconven-
ience, stumbling over ferns. I do not want to be ec-

centric, to use myself in that way. To fear the bourgeois is bourgeois.

The handsome white-haired couple who lived down the road in Ohio were natural bohemians. He (once a student of Adler and Jung), the last son of Austrian nobility: she, the daughter of commercial royalty, had discovered the arts. It was romance when they met in a Milwaukee bookshop where he worked.

Their house when I knew them was high-minded, low-budget modern, a theoretical plywood shack run down before it was finished. He lectured on American folk art with a singsong Baron Munchausen accent. She drifted through her plants, read Simone Weil and Martin Buber. Persian weaving, scraps of Mexican bark paintings were tacked to the walls. Birdseed and bread crumbs just outside the sliding glass doors: they watched the birds and the seasons in their half-acre of woods, slung a hammock to suggest ease between two willows that rooted in their septic tank. In late middle age they had produced a daughter, a strapping American girl. They were interested to see her drive off with boys in MG's and Porsches at thirteen. At fourteen she came into the living room where we sat drinking wine out of arty mugs and said: "I'm horny." Her parents were interested in that also, like two enchanted emigrés picking up the cheap wares in Woolworth's with curiosity.

Once they gave a dinner party for twenty people (the president of the university, deans, assorted luminaries). On the table with the crumbs from lunch this dear daft woman — hair rolled into a Grecian knot, hammered silver jewelry — set out a small canned ham and a few lettuce leaves. The president's wife, capable, patrician, found mustard and pickles in the refrigerator, opened cans of beans off the kitchen shelf. We all watched the birds in the snow pecking at seeds in the outdoor flood-light. Inside a Christmas tree was strung with cranber-ries and dull straw angels. For years our hostess had contemplated a translation of the letters of Kafka. Even as she talked, the letters were being issued in an official translation. Some blamed her for not giving us supper, but these two were protected by their incompetence, full of liberal goodwill. In the large sandy terrace that wrapped around the house she dug pits and buried the *New York Times* because she could not bear to throw it away. Termites thrived in the pulp.

Once, in secrecy, she entrusted me with a spiral notebook for a period of three days. I still remember her in my back yard under the maple tree — sharing with me — her innocent eyes excited by the prospect of the treasures I would find. In the notebook she had written: "There was a cruel scholar who made his wife and children sacrifice everything for his career. . . . A dominant woman is married to a quiet but brilliant doctor. . . . The son of a poor but noble European family travels to . . ." There were six or eight such précis laid out in simple declarative sentences, each story no more than half a paragraph and while I had the precious notebook in my care I might copy out any that I wished to use in my work. Chance of a lifetime. For two days I was overcome with alternate seizures of laughter and despair and on the third day returned the notebook with thanks. She was generous: it was all that she had learned from life. The cruel scholar died. The quiet doctor divorced. The son of a poor but noble family traveled to America where he met the daughter of a brewer in a Milwaukee bookshop.

There is no expression in the mirror that I will admit to — I cannot be that weary, my face growing to the waning look of my mother, my grandmother, and yet obscenely young with the big open grin of a Bridgeport hick. At my age bouncing around the Village is indecent, smiling at the janitors on my block. Last week I skipped rope, double-dutch, with office girls having fun on Thirteenth Street. Look, in this large mirror (once the splendid encasement for a valueless lithograph, cleaned-up version of *Marriage à la Mode* which hung in the "master" bedroom on North Avenue) and you will see that with the sack of expensive make-up, the good haircut, the pearls and my first Tiffany earrings I am as dull as the picture I ripped out of the frame, dull as the idea of a mirror over the couch. Impersonation of wife and mother: I have begun to wonder what I am like in real life.

Turn on the end of the game. They've gone into overtime, the fourth game this season they've done this to me—holding back the talent, sons of bitches. All right, they win but would it hurt them to give me a comfortable margin?

I will have a whiskey and soda, the only thing that will put me to sleep tonight. I'd like to admit that I don't understand your definition of the Sublime. I may have a fatal resistance to abstractions. It's perfectly clear that my attraction to the particular, the poignant, damns me in your eyes. Well, I mean more than I say.

The purple people were out riding today. Now they
have purple bicycles and purple sneakers. Thrilling
when they find some new purple thing they need,
shoelaces, handbags. I'm not sure I could live out of
the city. It's not available to me—the big scenes: Helle-
spont, Prince of Denmark, Khartoum, Camille, Fran-
cesca da Rimini, Easter 1916, Saint Catherine of
Siena, Sherman's March to the Sea. No God's heaven.
I can learn only the simpler subway routes. At least
once a month I end up in Queens or find myself in
papayas and breadfruit on Flatbush Avenue heading
for Grand Army Plaza. When I get off the train in
Union Square I come out at different exits each time,
unable to determine my fate among the passageways of
newsstands, florists, cheap leather goods, orange juice
fountains. I hate myself as the bewildered lady in from
Connecticut or the unworldly artiste. I need to find my
way home in rush hour. I need to take risks, not hail a
cab and take my ease, tipping according to the rules.
You see that I have lost my nerve and cannot go on.

On the other hand I've had the sense of myself in
recent years standing naked in the wings without embarrassment. It is a fearless dream in which I am
pressed at the last moment into the coloratura's role.
The set is constructed of Roman columns, French
armchairs and a gold-rush bar from Virginia City, Ne-
vada. I tack up a pressed-wood colonial eagle to make
the place my own, then turn to the audience, a capac-
ity crowd, and sing.

On the island of Nantucket there are six colors de-
creed by ordinance which may be used to paint the
shutters and doors of houses. The spectrum shrunk to
fulfill the dictates of good taste become morality. *They*

may be wrong. Let's not have that argument again about truth. I stayed up nights with that stuff in college. Forgive me . . . I concede I've dragged down to a personal level. . . . Oh, I wish I was as certain of the end of all your troubles . . . I am certain of nothing but of the holiness of the heart's affections. . . . For me the truth can never be a consensus of opinion. *They* may be wrong. I hold hopelessly, irrationally to absolutes. I believe in the mute, inglorious Milton and the madman who even now, unknown to the experts, is imagining the world again.

I will play my game until I am wiped out by words become lies, overcome with a blinding psychic emptiness like the loss of a child in the womb. Tomorrow I will huddle on the bed listening to the scalding cries of the disaffected couple downstairs (not six months married) or to the soprano on Ninth Street who has trilled the same scales, flat but with hope, for ten years . . . and so propped by my pillows, next to the phone, I will look across into the mirror at *that* story and turn back into the dream.

I meant to tell my daughter before she fell asleep with the radio blaring that it's okay to eat humble pie, but she must never accept stale bread. In the evenings I must stay at home and set the table as I see fit. The domestic metaphor suits me. Take the flowers away. Salt, pepper, ketchup bottle. Suppers will be homemade, fresh: There are signs of life.

II

MONEY

George Burns

I HAVE ALWAYS THOUGHT that my grandfather, for the purposes of his story, couldn't have had a better start in the world. As a small boy he was forced to quit school when his father went blind and take the reins, literally, of the family business. Together they drove the streets of Bridgeport with a single horse and delivery wagon, carting and hauling for any storekeeper or small manufacturer in need of their service. At home there were two sisters, Minnie and Mae, and his beloved mother, a true survivor with a ramrod back and faith as blind as the old man's eyes. She had worked as a housemaid for a Protestant family, a Mr. and Mrs. William Abbott Parrott, who owned a paint and varnish company in the North End.

When his father died my grandfather was set to work at a harness and livery shop owned by his uncle, Walter Stapleton, who humiliated him. One day when the boy displeased him, Stapleton took a horsewhip

and thrashed him severely. My grandfather said nothing but walked out of the place. Some fifty years later,
when I was growing up, we did not speak to the Staple-
tons. If, by a twist of fate, I were to meet any of that
clan, say at a cocktail party in Fairfield or on one of
my last trips to Bridgeport to settle my mother's estate,
it would still satisfy me to cut them dead.

There is a hiatus and when my grandfather reap-
pears it is as a grown man. He has carted and hauled
his way up in the world, learned the contracting business from a fine Yankee, Bradford Pierce, and now
stands in front of a long low stable on Thompson
Street with his crew, about twenty sturdy men in caps
and rumpled mismatched suit jackets. George Burns,
himself, is an impressive figure—tall, full-chested, a
stern, handsome Irishman in a well-cut Chesterfield
and derby hat. Next to him, in knickers with his black
head nearly shaved, stands a young Italian boy named
Giuseppe. There are half a dozen powerful horses and
freshly painted wagons in front of the stable and in the
background three brutally plain frame houses. On the
porch of the largest house a group of women in austere
dresses cluster behind a row of little children — his
family. One of the houses has been built for his mother
and sister Minnie, a pathologically shy woman who
will stay at home doing fine needlework and praying
for the rest of her days. The second little house is for
foolish Mae, who has married a drunkard named
Walsh, brought three children into the world and has
mercifully been abandoned. His own wife, Josie, and
his two children stand a hairs-breadth apart from the
rest. My grandfather feeds, clothes and houses all of

these people. He buys their coal and pays their doctor's
bills without blinking an eye.

He had contracted jobs all over New England, laid
railroad spurs in New Jersey and built the foundations
for the library and town hall in Greenwich down near
the state line. He had laid the flagstone walks at Amherst College and supplied feed to the Barnum and
Bailey Show, which had its winter quarters in the
South End. Now, in 1905, George Burns had figured
out that the automobile was more than a curiosity —
every house in the city would soon want a solid driveway. There were roads to be paved and new granite
curbs to be set all the way from Seaside Park to the
new fountain in the traffic circle downtown, a fountain
designed by Gutzon Borglum, the sculptor who was to
conceive Mount Rushmore: it looked like a soapdish
with a bronze mermaid saluting the hub of State
Street, Fairfield and Park Avenues. As the grid of side
streets was laid on the growing city there were new
roads to be cut through vacant lots — my grandfather
had more work than he could handle and there was
nothing he loved more than his work. Early every
morning he was up with his men and his horses. Making money was pleasurable and good. He liked his
name on the side of a new wagon, his signature on the
title to a house or a piece of land. He was partial to
corner lots. On the first of each month he went to
collect his rents, rolling the eight or ten dollars into
small brown salary envelopes used by the Burns Company and paying a short social call on his tenants, who
were all Irish and German.

When he was established, George Burns had married a Miss Josephine Baltis of New York City, a sprightly redhead who came up to the country — Bridgeport, that is — to visit relatives. That New York girl caught his eye: she was a grand dresser, played the piano and sang. Upon graduation from high school in 1876 she had received the highest honor, a gold medallion with her name, and had gone on to college for a year. When she met George Burns she was working in a big department store on Astor Place selling ribbons and lace. She was crazy for the opera and theater, the restaurants, but above all Josie loved the life in the city streets — Spring Street, Mott and Delancey. Her family owned a narrow wooden house and in the back yard kept a goat she found repulsive. When she was a blind old woman my grandmother confessed to me that she thought she would go mad when she first married: there were no crowds, nothing to see in Bridgeport and the quiet was terrible to her. Soon she could not fit into her blue silk wedding suit and she stopped gluing her fringe of bright hair to her forehead with gum tragacanth in the New York style.

Josie Baltis was the nearest thing to a gamble my grandfather ever took, but everything went right for him. She gave him a son and daughter in no time. Washing, ironing, baking bread, her days were as long as his. If she wasn't up with the children in the night, it was the horses. That was the remarkable thing, this smart city girl who had won a spelling bee for all Manhattan, who could sing the airs from Rossini and Strauss, had a gift with the horses and nursed them through colic. She was good with the workmen and the neighbors. Though my grandmother was Irish, born Darby, her widowed mother had remarried a kindly Mr. Baltis and she grew up with his name, speaking German. She made sauerbraten, wurst with kraut, apfelkuchen. Her admiration for her husband and his money was unbounded. In a silk top hat he was elevated to the Grand Knights of Columbus. She starched his dress shirts with reverence. Next he was appointed Fire Commissioner of Bridgeport. Every worthy fire in the city rang on an alarm in her kitchen.

I have looked for the flaws but time has erased pride, arrogance, greed. These grandparents were gods. I find only confirmation of the good years before the First World War and full support of the myth that these were innocent people who prospered. No alcoholic beverage was served in their home. My grandfather took on the obligation of two young Italians, Joe and Tony, who worked in the stables. Joe, Giuseppe, was his special prize: an orphan, his legal name was written Joe Seppe because a heartless immigration official couldn't understand what the boy muttered for a last name.

Apocrypha: In the days when my grandfather started his paving business, toolboxes were brought to each building site in a coffin-size box and left for the duration of the job. Theft was uncommon. His boxes were painted bright yellow (THE BURNS CO. it read in bold inky black) and with good old American know-how he had extra boxes made up and placed them around town where he had no contract to build at all.

Or that my grandmother, in the early days when she longed for her New York, got on the night boat in Bridgeport, the steamship *Nutmeg* that would dock in the morning at the Forty-second Street pier. She settled into the bunk of her first-class cabin dreaming of the crowds on the Bowery and lower Broadway, of Wanamaker's and Lord and Taylor's, the opera she would no doubt attend at Madison Square Garden. Something was amiss in the boiler room and when she went out on deck in the morning eager for her beloved city there were the low factories and dull skyline of Bridgeport and she wept.

Fact: In 1911 George Burns made a killing when he sold a piece of land with negligible buildings (corner of Commercial Street and Grand) to the Board of Education for fourteen thousand dollars. One triumph in many. At this time my grandfather joined forces with a Mr. Ford who worked in the office of the City Engineers. Both men were active in politics, close to Mayor Dennis Mulvahill. Righteous, churchgoing men, they bought up for a song property which they knew was soon to be developed and sold it at considerable profit to the city. It was good business.

Chattel and Heirs

THEN IT WAS TIME to move on, to store the outmoded equipment in the Thompson Street stables and divide the frame house into apartments for the rent. The Burns Company was now established, bright yellow throughout, on an extensive piece of land with its own railroad siding, its own blacksmith shop and weigh station, an office building and two company houses on ample green lawns for Tony and Joe. Gravel pit. Sandpit. Dynamite shed. Up on a hill the great shafts and pulleys of the asphalt plant under a high yellow shed.

The epic proportions of eighty-seven horses, balanced ledgers, loyal men.

I wish someone had noted for art's sake — it is pure Chekhov — my grandfather's feelings when he bought the property on which he was to build his grandiose house from Mr. and Mrs. William Abbott Parrott, the faded Yankee gentility for whom his mother had served as the Irish maid. It was a hideous home the Burnses built, thick gummy gray stucco meant to last forever with acres of cement porch, a baronial sweep of sidewalk and a stunning double drive to a two-car garage. Inside, the house strained for beauty with Palladian arches, walnut paneling and fireplaces meant for an English Lord. The butler's pantry that would never see a butler was stocked with Haviland Limoges and Waterford crystal bought at the best department stores. The sideboard must have heavy silver plate, empty decanters and in its drawers double-damask tablecloths for banquets never held. The furniture was quality Grand Rapids. Good Oriental rugs slid on the floors. They had everything, everything — punch cups for fifty, upright Steinway piano, bronze statue of *The Angelus*, a monstrous grandfather clock with Westminster chimes, gloomy moon, goon-faced sun rising across a hand-painted scene of the Rhine. At the top of the stairs a magnificent stained-glass window flaunted the purple water lilies of tag-end Art Nouveau.

The Burns's house sat across from a major railway crossing. One block up, the new Wonder Bread factory steeped the air daily with its yeasty smell. Mr. Kohler's butcher shop, so handy, was right on the corner. They had no claim to society other than the family, their tenants, their neighbors. It seemed the worst folly to

them — those Irish who moved out to Clinton Avenue
and Brooklawn Park near to the country club, edging
to the Fairfield town line. A man should be near his
horses and his men, near his asphalt plant.

Once a year in the off-season my grandfather traveled. Taking the Twentieth Century Limited from
Grand Central, he arrived in Chicago and bought his
workhorses from dealers throughout the Midwest.
When his business was done he went to Peacock's and
purchased tasteful jewelry for his wife and daughter,
cameos, diamonds and pearls, and once, it is the one
openly vulgar thing I know about him, he bought himself a whopper of a diamond ring, three big headlights
set in gold to flash in the eyes of the world.

A disappointment he could never explain: George
Burns, Jr., was a shiftless rich man's son. My grandfather drove down to Seaside Park, grabbed him by the
scruff of the neck and deposited him in the classroom
at Central High, a stupid, handsome, popular boy. But
the girl, Loretta, was near perfect, shy and fierce-
bright, pleasing her parents at every turn. Her father
could not help but buy her horses. She wore a trim
brown derby hat, a checked riding skirt and carried a
finely braided leather whip with a brass grip. There was
no place to ride — oh, up around the asphalt plant,
jumping the oil barrels or, sidesaddle, alone on the
bridle path in Beardsley Park. Once before she went to
college she rode up to Trumbull on her last horse,
named Billy F, miles and miles up into the hinterlands
with dirt roads and farmhouses: it stayed in her head
forever as the illicit, wild thing that she had done.

Life in the big house was much grander than my

mother expected, though her father caught her with a pot of rouge and scrubbed her face under the faucet with laundry soap. A presumptuous boy dared to come call on her with a box of chocolates. No one was good enough for her. She had everything: an initialed ivory hair receiver and nail buffer on a mahogany dressing table of her own, silk bed bolsters, embroidered sheets. My mother as an adolescent: I find a docile nouveau riche princess imprisoned in a hideous stucco castle playing the piano, doing Latin homework, giggling with a few girlfriends. That uninteresting good girl cannot exist apart from my memories of the embarrassed woman whom we had to force to open her Christmas presents. Often she would leave the room to baste the turkey or flute a pie rather than go through the agony of receiving a sweater or scarf. "It's not for me," she would say. I have a clear picture of my mother in the winter of 1942 after her bout with pneumonia. Thin and suddenly gray, she tries on a much-needed wool bathrobe fresh from its wrappings. A feverish blush rises on her neck and face. Her eyes tear up with shame.

She was given everything in her father's new house — a deep closet full of the best middy blouses and serge skirts. A sealskin coat with a youthful stone marten collar. Broad-brimmed hats dripping grapes and cabbage roses, white dresses of great delicacy meant to launch a young lady into society and which she simply wore down the street to High Mass at Saint Patrick's Church. How could she deserve the silk stockings, the silver hairbrush, the diamond lavaliere? By what right was she entitled to ride out in her father's new car wearing a full-length linen duster, amber gog-

gles and a costly high-crowned hat from Knox on Fifth
Avenue, a big beautiful Peg o' My Heart straw hat.

At Smith College she was homesick but stuck it out.
She dare not disappoint her father. One of the social
clubs was called the AOH, mocking the Ancient Order
of Hibernians, and the members took shanty Irish
names — Mudeater O'Climint and Annie Rooney
Terhune. She made tea dates and went on happy walks
with a few friends. In the name of the Burns family she
read Heine and Schiller, *Faust* and more *Faust*. The
answers to mathematical problems that no one could
solve in class came to her in her dreams.

I OWN A CURIOUS BOOK — *The Car of 1911: Being
the Latest Edition of the Locomobile Book, Which Illus-
trates and Describes 1911 Locomobile Models and Sets
Forth by Word and Picture the Many Varied Advan-
tages of the Locomobile Car.* It is handsomely bound in
a cover richly embossed with stylized acanthus leaves
and printed on thick rag paper. Until recently I had
always thought of it as a bit of nostalgia, on the order
of my Shirley Temple cereal bowl or the green tin
Lucky Strike cigarette box that hangs around my living
room with its campy charm. I had further been
disgusted with myself for giving the book shelf room,
hating the way in which the sentimental can diminish
the past, make it all too cute and easily comprehen-
sible. But the *Locomobile Book*, now that I have cared
to read it, is more than a kitschy item, more than a

family memento of limited appeal. It is an impassioned historical document, a dignified last stand for quality and workmanship against the sleaze of Ford and Chrysler that had begun to swamp the automotive market. There is a sad resignation in the stuffy prose: "The Locomobile plant enjoys what is probably the most beautiful location of any factory in the country, being situated on the edge of Long Island Sound at Bridgeport, Conn., adjoining Seaside Park."

The mode is industrial-pastoral — the air and sunshine provided for the workers, the orderly layout of the factory, every gear and bearing described in warm detail:

The cylinders are bored with great care, the cutting tools moving very slowly so as not to distort the cylinder walls, and three cuts are taken, the cylinders being aged between cuts. The final operation of cylinder grinding leaves the inside walls absolutely and permanently true with a hard glassy finish.

But who cared? Who really wanted that perfection described in "Chapter Twelve: Rear Axle and Shaft Drive System," or the durable brassbound running board or the transmission case of manganese bronze. The car was hopelessly expensive, a doomed object like the Fabergé eggs of a Russian prince. And who, in the heady prosperity that preceded the First World War had time to respond to the restrained pride of the Locomobile Company's boast: "We have always built our own engines."

The book contains unsolicited endorsements from delighted owners as far away as Wiesbaden and North Yakima, Wash. There is even a heroine, one that my

grandfather would have understood better than any
heroine in the novels he never read, the plays he never
saw — a Mrs. Harriet Clark Fisher, the active man-
ager of her own anvil works in Trenton, New Jersey,
who drove round the world in her Locomobile. Travel-
ing with her cook, Albert Bachellor; Maria, the Italian
maid; and Honk-Honk, a Boston bull terrier, she com-
pleted her adventures in a year and one month lacking
three days. In Ceylon they picked up Billykins, a mi-
nute monkey. It is all so foolish, crossing the Fuiji
Rapids on a raft, the blowouts in Utah. Mrs. Fisher
playing pioneer with her millions. In the Indian prov-
ince ruled by Sir Prabnu Narayan Singh, she was carried by four liveried servants in a "dandy" and placed
on a private yacht, ferried across the Ganges to the
marble landing leading up to the palace. "The landing
and steps were covered with red velvet, and during
Mrs. Fisher's entire visit to the potentate her feet were
not permitted to touch the earth."

We find her at the end, speaking of her "journey
through fairyland" and her "charmed life." There is no
poverty or squalor 'round the world. A fat widow, Mrs.
Fisher stands midst her souvenirs looking out the window of the anvil works on the flourishing cornfield by
the Delaware River where she hopes, magnificently, to
build homes for all her men and their families. There
are no trade unions, no anarchists, nor is there any
child labor in the land. It is the willed romance of the
early twentieth century.

Thus my grandfather, provincial patriarch, Diamond Jim Brady of Bridgeport, bought the local prod-
uct — a "48" Locomobile Type "M," Six Cylinder,
Shaft Drive Touring Car for forty-six hundred dollars.

Handsome appointments throughout: luxurious uphol-
tery of tufted tan morocco leather; windows of the
best French plate glass provided with silk curtains and
spring rollers of a shade to correspond. Despite all pre-
tensions to simplicity and their stunted social horizons
I find my grandparents looking rather haughty in a
photograph taken in the double driveway. George
Burns and Josephine (gone stout and dowdy Bridgeport) sit in the Locomobile swollen with their riches.
In the back seat of "the supreme American machine"
my worthless uncle and my mother look dutiful and
bored.

ASPHALT IS AS SIMPLE to make as cookies. Two fun-
nels lead to a large mixing bowl. The residue of petro-
leum is poured into one funnel, sand or fine gravel
into the other depending upon the consistency desired.
The batter is churned over heat and when it is well
blended it falls in a thick load into the waiting truck
like hot shit.

MY UNCLE GEORGE lounged downtown with the local
athletes. Josephine did her best to protect her son from
his father's wrath, but she couldn't get him up out of
bed to go to the Burns Company. A bit of fluff, a Miss

Margaret Kean, attracted the wastrel. She was fluttery-
sweet, insubstantial, poor and the decision was made
that young George should see the world. They shipped
him off in 1915 on one of the first steamers in Teddy
Roosevelt's Great White Fleet headed through the
Panama Canal. True, there was a rumor of war in
Europe — still, it is perfect that my grandfather did
not choose a transatlantic crossing to cool his son's
ardor. The engineering feat of the Canal with its
smooth locks and mighty Roebling cables, its promise
of an ideal commercial unity between the Hemi-
spheres, appealed more than Alpine views or French
cathedrals. Uncle George kept the dullest diary I've
ever read. After weeks on board of heavy meals, poker
games, good chat with faceless, sexless passengers, he
arrived in San Francisco with no particular interest,
plodded to Yellowstone, Dubuque, Kansas City, Chicago, and ran the last lap home into the arms of his
beloved. Their impetuous marriage was annulled by
the flu epidemic of 1918. In one night my uncle died.
His widow was set to work over the ledgers and yellow
billing system of the Burns Company. Across the double drive an enormous three-family house was built
which my grandfather signed over to her name and
there my Aunt Margaret lived in one of the flats, trem-
ulous and grateful.

In the role of the educated promising daughter my
mother failed. Her father had really wanted a safe local
schoolteacher, an aging girl correcting papers up in her
maidenly room. She painted roses on a whole unnec-
essary set of china. She was supplied with Ford run-
abouts but still forbidden to wear powder and rouge.

But it was her own money in the Bridgeport Savings Bank. Her precious bankbook of simulated maroon leather bore her account number, her own name. Over the years she treated herself to nice clothes and sometimes drove to New Haven with the other teachers to see a play. Her father's men bowed to her. Tony and Joe, who had almost been playmates, shuffled in front of this gentle schoolmarm, their caps in their hands. There were no horses anymore at the company — trucks, rollers, grading machines stood in the yellow stalls. Billy F, too old, roamed the field by the dynamite shed.

At thirty-three, when it seemed impossible, my mother fell passionately in love. The man had no money, hardly a steady job. He was like an actor with a beautiful voice. All night his stories about the wounded in France, about the gang at the courthouse where he was now a reporter. Everything was wrong with him. He was a four-flusher, had a temper, a store of foul language, a cleverness that would come to nothing. He was several years younger. She loved him. He could not live without her fineness and her submission.

George Burns said over my dead body and had a massive stroke on the left side. My mother helped feed him, wiped the spittle off his mouth, exercised his paralyzed leg and stole out at night through the cellar door to meet her man. She lied and cheated to be with Bill Kearns and married him against the old man's will. No wedding dress, no flowers: their vows exchanged in the basement of Saint Patrick's Church before a few schoolteachers and young reporters from the *Bridgeport Post*. They set up house out of the maroon bankbook in a lowly flat above the poor Kearnses on the East Side. My grandfather, godlike, forgave them and in a year he had sold my father and mother his side yard for a dollar. There in the shadow of his stucco manse (the bleak expanse of his cement porch was to hover above our 1930's sun parlor) my parents built their dream cottage with tiny rooms, cramped closets, cute Tudor hinges and doorknobs. In front they looked out on a new all-night diner, while in the rear Aunt Margaret's gray three-family monster faced them beyond the garage and double driveway. That shingled peak-roofed cottage, about the size of Joe and Tony's company houses, is where we grew up. It was called, predictably, the little house.

I HAVE ONLY ONE memory of my grandfather Burns that is my own, not legend. I am very small, maybe two years old playing in the paneled dining room of his house. He is a heavy white-haired man half reclining in a morris chair. I see him in felt slippers and one of those old shirts without a collar. Each time he speaks his garbled message my grandmother repeats the words clearly.

"Ge-th-pens. Ge-th-pens," he commands with a flailing of his good arm.

She goes through the swinging door of the butler's pantry and returns with a jar of pennies all of which he gives to me.

For twenty years after his death Josephine Burns stalked the rooms of her house in mourning. Black lace-up shoes, black cane after her broken hip. Black dresses, black sateen aprons and a wad of cash in a flannel petticoat up under her skirt. Her back hunched up and over. White hair in a tight bun. The linen shades rotted on the windows, armchairs faded, faucets dripped rust stains in all the sinks. A talented girl in the neighborhood came to practice on the Steinway. Giuseppe arrived at the back door in fealty with vegetables and flowers and gallons of his homemade wine. After the wine turned to vinegar my grandmother poured it down the sink. She was said to be a wonderful woman. I certainly thought so because I spent hours in that empty mausoleum reading in the quiet, and at any time I could amuse myself by poking through the funny hats and discarded diamonds. I suppose she was wonderful because she prayed eternally and huddled near the radio on Saturday afternoons to hear the opera. She was sweet-tempered, dignified, entirely private and thought to be rich. When her eyes scummed over with cataracts she was brought to sleep with us next door in the little house and led back home in the morning, there to spend the day literally feeling the way around her possessions.

GOD, WASN'T THE Depression fun. Don't forget it. The scrimping and saving. Living on my father's salary. Nests of money stashed away for the United Illuminating Company, Southern New England Telephone, Hoffman Fuel. Good days — the money eked out for dancing lessons or a trip to the movies. My mother half dead after a day's housework, rolling out pie dough. The holy sacrifice of a quarter when an unemployed man came to the door selling aprons or pot holders made by his wife. Having the poor kids from Parrott Avenue in for a "real" party with store-bought games and fancy ice-cream molds. What a sham. Fretting that we could not afford what my grandmother would surely give us — good winter coats, tuition to the Jesuits and Sisters of Mercy, a silver-gray Packard or a Lincoln Continental.

But I've sped by the carefree hard-luck days of the thirties to pathology, the diseased attitude toward money that would last my parents the rest of their lives. About the time Franklin Roosevelt took office they decided to pretend in our let's-pretend cottage that we could not move to a neighborhood with shade trees and lawns, that we must shop for our underwear in Engleman's dingy dry-goods store, that we did not spend a fortune on heavy cream, lamb chops and steak. Let's pretend that at any rational moment Loretta and Bill couldn't have forced the sale of a piece of property, God knows there was enough of it. And why, so queer, did my grandmother dig up into her petticoats for dollar bills? Why did George Burns's diamond ring, appraised at six thousand dollars, clunk around the bottom of a cracked sugar bowl in our pantry for years while my brother worked his ass off in a bursar's job at Yale and I went to Smith with humiliating clothes stitched up on my mother's sewing machine — skirts with lumpy pleats, the arm of one jacket awry, set in so amateurishly that I looked as if I'd had major surgery of the right breast.

For years my mother said we were like that penniless family in George S. Kaufman's *You Can't Take It with You*, fancy-free bohemians, and for years I believed her. My parents were enchanted by their supposed poverty. I was a grown woman when I understood with considerable pain that they had lied to me. The jolly times in our little house were dishonest, thus spoiled forever. I had forced this discovery during a bad time when I was attending to my life. I was full of answers and furious. My father was three years in his deluxe copper-lined coffin in Saint Michael's Cemetery and my mother's hold on the facts was daily more fragile. So my brother and I went at it one night — how they had cheated us of good English bikes and tennis lessons that we never really wanted, how often they had made us feel like slum children dressed up for a party, how I had gone to work in the public library the day I reached sixteen because I honestly thought they needed my paycheck and it was a joke to them, how George worked long summers over loads of hot asphalt far below the union wage. Our bitterness which lasted till dawn was thoroughly satisfying. Since then we have never talked of our family's warped attitude toward money except in the lightest vein, for we know we've inherited it along with their rugs and lamps. It helps to soften the anguish now to see that we had to live through the Depression in our little house: in those years my mother was free. She was not beholden to her father. For twenty years the salary check from the state of

Connecticut came each month as a ticket of indepen-
dence and, we must believe, set no limit on domestic
bliss.

After the Ball

THE HEAVY COMMENTARY of events: when my grandmother was at last blind and incontinent we moved
into the ugly stucco house to nurse her. With new curtains and wallpaper there was a momentary cheer but
even with my mother's Japanese flower arrangements
and two television sets the place was never home to
me. We presumed upon the glories of the past. My
bedroom in that house still stored the dress shirts of
dead men, buttonhooks, postcards of the Grand Pier in
Atlantic City and Old Faithful shooting off. (When I
moved a half-dozen times during the first years of my
marriage it particularly angered my parents. A house in
Knightsbridge, a summer sublet in New York, the upstairs of a Victorian house in Ohio, Viale Porta Latina,
Rome. My father said of us: "They don't have a pot to
piss in.") They had left their shingled make-believe
cottage and never looked back across the alley. Though
my parents settled into the big rooms with a proprietary
air, the high ceilings and fancy woodwork seemed to
take possession of them.

My mother fell in love with the hallway arches and
stained-glass windows once again, the Westminster
chimes on the half-hour, the black iron cooking range
and the gleaming copper water heater in the kitchen. It
was all hers. She showed the rooms of the house to visitors as though they were of historical interest, the pal-

ace of a fire commissioner, circa 1910. She displayed
her sidesaddle to my friends and with some irony
showed the Installation Program for the Easter Banquet
at the Knights of Columbus: Bluepoint Oysters followed by Monsignor John Gannon, Prime Ribs of Beef
au Jus, the Right Honorable Dennis Mulvahill, Potatoes O'Brien, etc. *They* knew how to live. Here was a
top hat cradled in its own leather case. Here a tortoise-
shell shoehorn, two dozen butter plates, motoring
goggles, mourning veils, this menu with a red tassel
from Delmonico's. As yet there was nothing ghastly
about these artifacts. Her audience could always detect
the touch of self-deprecation: she assumed her schoolteacher's smile that told us no one of our generation
could quite understand the thrilling fourth book of the
Aeneid or the grand scale of her father's career.

THE STORY ENDS with a number of melodramatic
scenes to balance the opening shot of the blind man
with his plucky son guiding him through the crowded
streets of downtown Bridgeport. First, we are driving
around the defunct Burns Company with an eight mil-
limeter camera, George, Jack Ennis, Mary Ruth —
the most beautiful of my old high school friends —
and other playmates. Our idea is a parody chase
sequence to be followed by lust and murder. We have
a serape and ten-gallon hat, an evening cape and so
forth in the car. No doubt a good supply of beer. My
brother, who remembers none of this, is trying to get

the right tilt to the car as he swings around the office building and suddenly there is a shriveled dark figure stumbling down the hill from the plant, an ancient man in mismatched suit jacket and pants running after the car, waving his gray cap.

"Georgie, Georgie," he cries. It is Joe, Giuseppe, and he holds to the window of the car, clutches the steering wheel to stop our games. "Georgie," he says, "why you no come and save you grandpa's land?" As he continues to plead with us in broken English tears wash down the old man's cheeks and he is suddenly ashamed.

IN THE EARLY SIXTIES when I am home on a summer visit vandals set fire to the company. Everything in flames — the stables, blacksmith shop, barns and asphalt plant — an ominous flare in the field near the empty dynamite shed. It is the end at last. My father, the excitement is said to be bad for his heart, stands beside the fire engines with Jasper McLevy, the former Socialist mayor. They are old men in suspenders, their clownish pants dangling from their dying bodies. Crowds come from all over the city. The neighborhood is blocked off, but my mother remains in her house fussing over plates and saucers, trying to speak a word or sing. The fire is a social occasion. Bill Kearns jokes with his old buddies from the Police Department and the Fire Chief. My father, the decent reactionary, and Jasper McLevy, the mild Bolshie, say that there are no men left of the caliber of George Burns. Together, they recall his full head of white hair and strong chest. They agree that the city was built with his honest vision and sturdy pride. Amen. The Burns Company is leveled by the holocaust. No, the charred yellow office and gas pump remain.

IN THE NOW-FILTHY kitchen of the big house the shelves with the everyday dishes are in confusion. Bottles of pills for innumerable ailments are stacked beside thimbles and shoelaces. It is too difficult for my mother to climb the stairs constantly and put things away. Tubes of Ben-Gay and rubbing alcohol attest to pain. In a cut-glass finger bowl my father's dental bridge rests in murky water. Among the Christmas cards and telephone bills I find nearly two thousand dollars of uncashed checks (social security and dividends) which I force them to sign and then deposit in the bank. This is only a preliminary to the horror that I come upon one day soon after my father's death. My mother is in the kitchen, quite happy at the sink scrubbing something in a red dishpan. It is ten- and twenty-dollar bills that she has washed furiously in strong detergent. Now she hangs them to dry in the dish drainer and over the towel rack.

"Mother, that's crazy."

"But the money is so dirty," she says.

When I call George he says, yes, of course, she's washing the bills. It is crazy and he hadn't wanted to tell me.

AT LAST A SPUR of Interstate 95 is slated to "take" the big house, the little house, and Aunt Margaret's monster. The crappy two-family houses down the street where the WPA workers and the poor kids lived will remain. No one of influence is left to buy off the Department of Highway Engineers. It takes me six weeks with my brother's help to shovel the junk out of the cellar and attic: the corpses of twenty radios, clam steamers and double boilers with the price tags still on, linen sheets and pillowcases in their original wrappings from the store, city directories, darkroom equipment, every note of condolence re: my uncle's death in the flu epidemic. My daughter, who is in kindergarten, plays with feather boas and corsets, trails lace curtains like wedding veils as she minces up and down the grand staircase in stained satin pumps: it is unhealthy.

Then we install my mother in a sunny and spacious apartment a half-mile from her home. She will never leave Bridgeport, yet she is a refugee in these flimsy rooms. There before her terrible end, she talks to new neighbors, walks to a new church, watches her television. When I visit she presses money on me, a sign of love. These rooms mean nothing to her. In great agitation she loses all the savings books and bonds three times a week and George gently takes them away.

Then she is content. You see, she has everything — the grandfather clock with the top chopped
off to fit the low ceiling, her riding skirt, an extra set of
headlights for the Locomobile. She has everything. In
a final apotheosis she roams the cramped apartment
touching Limoges, silver plate. Hanging on a door-
knob she finds her finely braided whip that urged Billy
F on to Trumbull. Out of a cookbook she produces her
own bankbook (canceled) of simulated maroon leather
which bears her name. Then she begins her rounds
again. Her fingers blue with the cold of age, she
touches hair receiver, German grammar, diamond
ring, Limoges, punch cups, silver plate. Here is a
signed receipt from the Barnum and Bailey Show,
1886. She has everything, everything.

AFTERWORD: we are in a depressed market at the moment of my inheritance. It's hell dealing with that
money, the pittance that is left, not the meaningless
list of stocks in the dwindling trust, but the doomed
monetary history of my family: my mother's guilt, my
father's subordinate role as the breadwinner in our
lives. I want to be as innocent as George Burns in the
story of his dramatic rise before the Great War. I want
the unselfconscious moment, maybe just a handful of
cash earned by my sweat that would not seem another
joke to them, a moment in which I would not stop to
think of their indulgent smiles.

When my brother and I sit in the lawyer's office discussing my mother's estate we must provide a diverting hour for that good man. George's voice drops to a serious timbre, rather like the old radio parodies of senators, but his sentences are high Dickensian, baroque, beginning and ending nowhere. They lend robust support to his ignorance. There is a pompous ruffling through his papers which, I observe with envy, are stuffed into an impressive metal strongbox. I have come with two shopping bags full of bank statements, appraisals, letters from the Judge of Probate, etc. My ruse is to take notes as though I am at a seminar in reality. I have memorized phrases like cash flow and growth investment. I am ready to exercise my options. Then I ask questions that have already been answered and my studious pose falls away. In much the same way I attend to my publisher. The effort is draining for me as he explains his budget and my royalty statements that might be written on papyrus for all I can decipher. The trick is not to let him know I don't understand and in any case it's over quickly like a minor dental appointment, then we can eat our lunch in peace.

I declare myself to be absolutely sane in the matter of paying bills. The last three times I overdrew my account it was proved the fault was not mine. I have driven ninety miles round trip to purchase a skirt and sweater at a ten-percent discount, written reviews for literary magazines at the rate of two cents an hour, pissed away twenty dollars in cab fares in one anxious day.

I have gone for the big money and failed, consorting with television people who would have me turn the life of Edith Wharton, our greatest woman writer, into

smut. On the theory that nothing is too vulgar — sell
yourself, honey — I have spent the most degrading day
of my life at a book-and-author luncheon. My delicately turned speech was a flop, preceded by a Las
Vegas show girl with dirty stories, followed by a brute
in cowboy boots and string tie. Here was fame and fortune: two hundred–plus housewives as my audience
drank daiquiris and Bloody Marys at eleven o'clock in
the morning around the glassed-in swimming pool of a
distinguished motel. There was something pure in the
utter filth of the experience. The cowboy, who wrote
sentimental children's stories, insulted those women:
"I'm not really an author, ladies. I'm a taster in a
prune juice factory. I work one day and I'm off three."
Yes, I was awake and breathing. I remember feeling
that I should rise, like a lady, and leave the room, or at
least transport myself with a tough assignment — think
of Dante, his grand scheme, or find the opening line
of *Pride and Prejudice,* try the Confiteor in Latin. "I'm
a donor to an artificial insemination bank," the cowboy said to his adoring women, " — a little dab'll do
ya, girls." The woman on my right explained that au-
thors were a big draw, next to the fashion show and
hair stylist in popularity. Thank God for her blather:
she told me the price of her son's stereo and of his car.
She told me her weekly budget for food, her mill rate
and the cubic feet in her house. So great was her greed
that she measured the air.

The signs are encouraging for the completion of a
business deal. A stranger will offer a big reward for my
efforts. Take a chance. I have saved $6.45 parboiling
string beans and placing them in my freezer in plastic

bags. The floppy violet paper I've thrown on my desk
with the junk mail is, I do realize after a week, funny
money, a stock certificate: Bristol Myers has split.

But let me play from my strength, before you take
me, or take me for a fool. Your driveway is poorly
graded, it ships water. The edges are not tamped . . .
let me give you my card. These unsightly seams left by
the roller will give in the frost . . . we have done
quality work since 1896. That apron in front of your
garage is a rotten job, but where the land slopes off
sharply I foresee real trouble . . . you should have a
berm, that is, a raised hillock of asphalt, so that you
will not drive with me straight into the abyss.

III
Sex

WHAT GOOD WILL IT DO if I tell you the truth? What purpose will it serve when you prefer distortions. Oh, you do — some nice story, or not so nice. Some story: how I'd never heard of a dildo before I was thirty. Can you believe that? And then, massaging my upper arm one day (bursitis, inflammation of the tendon, I never knew) it occurred to me, the shape of the thing pumping in my hand, dear God, and the sly man in the drugstore had tried to sell me a vibrating disk that cupped my shoulder. "No," I said, "I'll have this long one," and I stroked the thing, pleasing the shape. I slipped it back to him across the counter, into his antiseptic hands, clean nails, important wristwatch giving the time in Madrid, Los Angeles, Tel Aviv. We faced each other at Sixth Avenue and Eighth Street — aspirin, cough drops — ah, the shame of my innocent transaction, his finger playing in my palm. Dimes and quarters dealt to me slowly. Why that dirty laugh?

"Which arm is it?" he asked.

"The left," I said.

"Well, I hope your knee improves."

Fool, can you believe that? The joke's on me. Another instance of the self-mockery of an educated woman writing of sexual adventures. Cunt, they write, prick — isn't that grand? Risking nothing — every comfort station on the highway displaying their book jackets with glossy tits, golden asses. Searing, frank. Now it can be told — the story of your ordinary Ivy League English major making it. Making it on her back, just as she once scored on the college boards, riding high, cracking the exam in cunnilingus. Reward for one's effort: achieving orgasm. Sixty-nine percent of the women sampled achieved orgasm fifty-three to ninety percent of the time. Twenty-five percent of the ninnies were thinking of meat loaf or whether the slacks should match the blouse or the back talk they took from their adolescent kids. Six percent flunked, failed to achieve, so they must wander the earth as outcasts, their IBM cards punctured with the proof of their disgrace, while the girls in the honors seminar fondle their breasts, experiment with moist dewlaps. Accomplished in sensuality. They are telling each other, telling each other. That's more kicks than pricks, I imagine. And "fuck," they write, fantasies trapped in the old forms. Words ancient as stones serve them as they spread themselves to the world, all of it told, gone public, the suck and the fuck of it, the kiss, caress, yearning, refusal to yearn and summa, summa, summa they cry at climax. They have achieved.

It's clear that I am upset. No, angry. The truth is that I am afraid — here I will fail, not find the metaphor or the gesture, for I have always been convinced

that the great sex scenes, for me, are scenes that give
me knowledge of my own sexual life — the thwarted
suburban flirting in *Hedda Gabler*, sick old man
caressing the stocking leg of the silly young matron, or
Elenya, languidly twisting up her hair in *Uncle
Vanya*, displaying herself in front of the impotent,
then dallying with the only man onstage so that she
may close out the man in him. Or those drunken
Irishmen in O'Neill with their whores and their saintly
wives-mothers-sweethearts and their crippling romantic
sob stories. . . . So, I have created another evasion,
but look when I take off my glasses and open the top
three buttons on my blouse, wet my lips slightly with
the tip of my tongue. I'm ready if you are.

First Love: A Limited View

COME STAND WITH ME by the dining room window.
Under the sill there is a cream-colored radiator with a
metal top grained to look like wood. It is a strange
place in the house, not private, not central. I am waiting for my father's car to turn into our driveway. It is
dark early on these winter nights and I have turned the
back-porch light on to welcome him. Now, past suppertime, my mother calls me — we will eat without
him. She is afraid the meat will dry out, but I will not
come to the table. It is cold: as I count the cars that
pass, my forehead chills against the upper window
pane. All sensibility and sorrow, I keep my vigil. My
father may be dead, slumped over the steering wheel
on a back road. He is the Detective of Fairfield County
and it is true, there are guns and handcuffs in the

drawer of our buffet, yet I'm forcing my emotions.
Blood may be soaking from his wound, through his
shirt and vest. My mother is so unworthy, eating lamb
chops with George.

Stand with me by the window. Here we can see everything — the back of my grandfather's stucco house
with cold stone steps down to cellar darkness crawling
with real spiders and imagined snakes. Across the
driveway my aunt's house: widowed early she is now
surrounded by her sisters, upstairs and down, all of
them scurrying to daily Mass, all of them tippling
sweet manhattans. To the right behind the lordly two-
car garage lies the Schaaks's garden tended by their two
girls.

The Schaak girls were middle-aged women: Clara
who courted for twenty years, swung on the porch with
her gray-haired suitor, Willy, stuffed him with homemade sauerkraut and dumplings. Then she laughed all
evening, coarse and hearty, while he swatted her pair
of nippy little dogs from his ankles. Madeleine Schaak,
the older one, gone deaf as a stone before she got her
man, then gone crazy, teaching her junior high class
nothing, hearing nothing while the fresh kids spoke
obscenities aloud in the last row. Finally, responding
to the shouts of the world she plugged her ear with a
flesh-colored device, wires strung into her big old
boobs, and she drew me into their house one day. It
was clean and ugly in all aspects. There she showed
me her extensive collection of Royal Doulton
figurines.

Well, she had that, didn't she? She had the lady
selling balloons and the ballerina and girl with parasol,
the whole catalogue. Some she had bought herself and

some were presents from her boyfriend, the man who got away.

"You should learn to love beautiful things," she shouted. Madeleine was so angry and shrill. I shouted back that they were lovely, especially the girl in the hoopskirt.

"She is called Girl on a Windy Hill. I paid for her myself."

Meanwhile, in a bedroom down the hall, the mother, bossy and strong-willed as a Wagnerian fury, refused to die and that is why Madeleine could not marry all those years while she could hear. Some of her figurines were birds made to look real in every detail. I had to wait there and talk about their feathers and beaks and then she asked me about a school friend, a particular girl who was the niece of Connie Ryan, the man who got away. I had been brought into that ugly parlor to say things about that girl and whether I ever saw Con Ryan — if he ever gave us a ride or took us to the movies.

"Does he have a ladyfriend?" she asked.

There was nothing to fear but a stout woman with watery eyes and faded hair pulled down to hide (it did not hide) the hearing aid: I did not know whom I might betray.

I said, "The birds are my favorite . . ."

"Well, if you like beautiful things you better learn to pay for them yourself." Madeleine Schaak laughed, clutching the wires down to her bosom, and released me to my childish ignorance. After that she talked to me over the fence about the weather, the size of her dumb heavy-headed dahlias and frost-green cabbages in their garden, and of her mother's phlebitis.

The old woman died. Wearing wine wool crepe and matching toque, Clara Schaak married Willy, who all these years had a last name: "Clara, daughter of the late Herman and Flora Schaak, will continue as receptionist at Watkins Optical, 530 Main St." Some romance. They moved to a small house in Stratford near the Sound, fished on weekends.

"They have a life," my mother said.

I understood that. They lived together, fat Clara and Willy, coarsely laughing, fishing, eating what they pleased in their own house. I understood, too, that they had a sexual life, wine wool crepe and gray hair notwithstanding. Loyal lovers through mutual dentures and Willy's shoe cut out round the bunions, they waved to me when they visited Madeleine on Sunday in these happy days. Expansive now, they played cards with a group in their development. They were granted one year.

Maddened with envy, Madeleine ripped the hearing aid out of her ear, let her class riot. She drove in lonely silence against the traffic horns and police whistles, striking out at the whole noisy world. She staggered up the steps of her porch not hearing her own shuffle. The quiet was a conspiracy; the walls bounced her, threw her off balance to the bathroom floor. Crippled and crazy, she was taken to the second bedroom in Stratford by Clara and Willy with her Royal Doulton collection and a monthly retirement check.

"Cornelius Ryan broke her heart." Even my mother's tone had a note of cynicism.

"Well, he did," I said.

"Don't be a fool," my father laughed. "Con Ryan

lives with his sisters. They give him pocket money. They wipe his ass."

"Bill —," my mother said.

"That foolish woman," he said, "in all those years he never laid a hand on her."

Thus the unhappy Schaak sisters. Some romance. But on the second floor of their house lived Blanche, Eddie and the boarder in perfect harmony. . . .

Waiting for my father by the back dining room window: an early memory flattened now by humdrum psychology, but how I yearned for him to turn in the drive, how I pushed to imagine his death, my loneliness. *She* would be sorry for washing up the plates and cutting her pie.

A white Persian cat bathes in the window up above the Schaaks' where Blanche, Eddie and the boarder eat dinner at the kitchen table. From here we can see everything and theirs is such a decent story: the cat was a curiosity in a neighborhood that did not run to thoroughbreds, but there was never a word of scandal about little Eddie, who came up to the tits on his wife and rode the bus to work at a desk in City Hall, while Big Blanche drove out with the boarder, a spare man who moved like a stick drawing. The boarder worked at a desk in a factory, dressed with care, opened the door for Blanche, carried her bundles. She made his lunch but not Eddie's, still they were a happy lot. Blanche had pretty feet and good legs that held up her large body. She was French, by which we meant French-Canadian, and therefore entitled to bright dresses, flowerpot hats, costume jewelry and an exotic indoor cat. It seemed to entitle her also to a lover. When we were little kids, George and I knew the boarder "did it" with Blanche, before we knew what it was they did. Every summer they went off on a vacation together and little Eddie, a cheerful gabber, obligingly took his meals at the Stratfield Hotel. He ate steaks and lobsters. He had the time of his life. The whole arrangement was pleasingly bourgeois. The neighborhood was indulgent and even in our house, so inflexible about liquor and debts, dirty pictures, there was a mysterious approval. From the back dining room window I could see the boarder on a Sunday back out his car to drive Blanche to Mass though he was not a Catholic. He waited outside church reading the paper and quite often they gave little Eddie a ride home.

Twenty-nine cars have turned into our street, but not his black Chevrolet. Now I am sure my father is dead. It is hopeless, waiting for him, but I would rather die hungry here by the window than go into the kitchen and eat. I will continue to think of him until the telephone rings with the awful news. The dimple in my father's chin will be shadowed with beard by this hour. The streetlamp picks out the Miklos's house across Parrott Avenue with the cruel glare of a searchlight. Mr. Miklos rented one of our garages and each night he padlocked the garage door with precision, turned and walked the driveway's length like a soldier, crossed the street and entered his house. There was something wrong with the teachings of the Church as I had learned them, for though Mr. Miklos was a saint among us, his home was purgatory. Mrs. Miklos sat in a chair in their middle room. All day and all night she sat in the chair. She did not go to bed. She did not go to the toilet — she sat in a squat armchair with papers spread on the floor for her like an animal.

Fanny, an old crone (aunt or cousin) who looked as though she needed a keeper herself, tended to her. Mr. Miklos brought her supper on a tray. He dressed her in large housecoats. He hired a woman to give her permanent waves. He changed her papers. Fred, their handsome son, was little help. He was a bully who played ball in the street, rode his bike after dark and when he did go in the house he yelled at his invalid mother. She yelled back.

My aunt and her sisters prayed for her recovery. There was great traffic in rosary beads and blessed candles. Mrs. Miklos sat in her chair surrounded by holy cards and statues. Two or three times I was taken to visit her, to watch her oozing in her chair, but my mother could not stand the sight herself and then we sent poinsettias and lilies on holidays. Mrs. Miklos had a baby voice, a baby face: "Fwed," she called her son, and wasn't I a darling.

"What's wrong with her? " I asked.

"Her body retains water," my mother said, but that was no answer at all. There were rumors: some time ago when my aunt went over to the Miklos's with a bowl of pudding, she'd seen her run around the dining room table after Fred and thrash him. Mrs. Miklos could walk: I remember how large this fact was. But Mrs. Miklos sat. It was all a lie, the prayers for the invalid, the flowers and pudding, the nods to the blank window where she sat looking out, growing more sodden in her festering chair.

I don't know how I pieced this story out, for no one would help me, yet I know it is true: after Fred was

born, Mrs. Miklos could not feed him. She would not
let Mr. Miklos into her room — someone let that slip.
She stayed in bed. The best they could ever do with
her was get her in that chair. Trauma. Case history.
Perhaps she was ashamed of what she'd done with her
tall Polish husband and saw Fred as the proof of her
sin. I can only speculate, but I know she was nursed
like a baby, cried and fretted in her chair which had
become part of her soft sexless body.

From time to time there were attempts at — no,
truly assaults upon — normality. Sitting still, Mrs.
Miklos would have my aunt to tea or receive Christmas
visitors. Once there was a birthday party for Fred and
though I was years younger I was forced to go. I was
forced to go because my mother had forgotten Mrs.
Miklos for so long and George had been pushed off his
bike and slapped around by Fred and those rough boys.
I was five years younger than the tarty high school girls
that day. Fred was already bragging about enlisting in
the army to give us a thrill. Ginger ale, grape soda,
plates of damp tuna and egg sandwiches in view of the
chair. Fanny and Mrs. Miklos joined the fun. The big
girls in sweaters and skirts, lipstick, nylons. The boys
in Sunday suits. Cheap pocketknives and ties for Fred.
Poppers and fortunes. I still had braids and a smocked
dress. I thought I would never forgive my mother for
not foreseeing this disaster.

In the mounting frenzy of ripped crepe paper,
spilled soda and burst balloons, Mrs. Miklos demanded
that we play post office or spin the bottle. I'm used to
seeing whores shoved into pimpmobiles on Eighth
Street, children selling themselves on Times Square.
Once some Yale men I knew put a condom on a blind

man's nose. Nothing compared to the sexual degrada-
tion of the green ginger-ale bottle spinning on the dining room table at Fred's birthday party and the orgy of
kissing, stroking, shrieking that Mrs. Miklos directed.
"Squeeze her good. Take her on the couch, Joe."
Maestro of French kisses, sneaky feel-ups, she con-
ducted from the chair. Twelve or thirteen, that was her
sexual age. At the time I felt safe. The green bottle was
controllable: none of those big boys wanted me.

But of course it happened. Fred spun and there I
was, a laugh with my braids. "Kiss her Fwed. She's shy.
Take her in the bedwoom." And so I was dragged into
the dark room where at night Mr. Miklos slept alone.
Fred kissed me. He meant no harm, a big lout who
would play basketball at Bassick High for a few years
and get a leg wound in the war.

There is a happy ending: she died. It was something
of a circus getting her to the hospital. My father and
Pat Deady helped the attendants from Saint Vincent's
heave her into the ambulance. Mr. Miklos survived to
marry a thin Polish widow of an appropriate age. He
moved away. That is a happy ending. So what if I
learned more than I was ready to take: false prayers,
septic wounds of the spirit. But I find that I have no
mercy for Mrs. Miklos: she wanted life to be spoiled for
us children at the birthday party as it was for her. She
wanted the reenactment of her dirty kisses. She wanted
to ruin our hugs and squeezes, to show us the filthy
games she'd played.

I know that I should set you aside, Mrs. Miklos,
from moral judgment as a psychotic, queen of the
neighborhood crazies. Perhaps I should be grateful.
Through you I come to Hieronymus Bosch, to much

of Faulkner and Flannery O'Connor, to Fellini and some of the best love scenes in Beckett. Through you I see the oldest male prostitute in the world as he leaves his house on my block with his cane (he is partially sighted), perfumed for his last trick but one. I know The Anvil, The Ramrod, The Toilet, the S-M bars in the West Village through you — and I know what goes on there, not out of Krafft-Ebing but out of the vision you gave me that day after Fred blew out the candles on his cake. Thanks for inviting me: I hope you are sitting forever, unable and untended, in your chair.

My prayers were answered as my father's car swung into the driveway. He appeared on the back walk whistling, pushing up his hat with his thumb, topcoat open. He was wearing my favorite brown herringbone suit and a striped tie. Whole and healthy, he explained to my mother what had kept him late. She said the furnace was making an odd squealing noise and set out his dinner and mine. He said the meat was dry, then called for the ice water he drank with all his meals: this was not the man I loved, but it was some romance.

Buddy Grote

A GAME PRECEDED the event, one of those games that has kids running through back yards, hiding breathless behind bushes or in doorways. We ran into his cellar, Buddy Grote and I. Being there in the dark we kissed. Third grade or fourth, while I still played with boys. Our faces were cold. His jacket was brown leather with a zipper and he wore a helmet with earflaps, the whole effect to seem an air force pilot. After kissing we wiped our mouths and went out to play. The smell and feel of his leather jacket remained with me for years, yet I didn't like him for any number of days. Our kisses were isolated from other childhood games, a discovery, and I did not feel that swelling of desire with such intensity again until I was an adolescent.

He was a squat German Catholic boy from a hardworking family, a dumb boy who could not pass his high school classes. When I was in college he used to talk to me on summer nights though he had no interest in me then. He'd become a pathological liar: standing out by the Parrott Avenue fence I was a new audience. His overwrought tales sounded like the plots of espionage movies or comic-book stuff. "Bam," Buddy Grote said. "This guy whammed me on the chin in front of the Polack bar. Pow. I got him in the belly." Like that — with sirens, quick getaways. A man of the world in his U.S. Marine Corps signet ring, privy to secrets of the FBI and the Coast Guard Patrol. There was a seething low life in the harbors of Bridgeport and Stratford, Connecticut, comparable to the intrigues of Casablanca or Marseilles. Dope, sex, "Wow" — this woman kicked him in the balls. Brass knuckles, bribes — all choppy free-running lies. Nothing connected. Sentences in clouds like Captain Marvel speech puffed out of the mouth. It was all so mad, sidling up to me at the side gate so the bad guys wouldn't hear. He worked as a night watchman at Raybestos and did have a fake badge and peaked cap. Sometimes George got caught with Buddy Grote, the zaps and wows, his schemes for making thousands or

the woman with dangerous connections hungering for
his body. In later years I heard Buddy was "sent away"
from time to time. He came to my mother's funeral
balding and sane with a frump of a wife, still a good-
looking boy, still a Catholic. We talked in whispers beside the bier about the old neighborhood, those who
had moved away, those who remained and what ailed
them. He led me a few steps off into the bank of
flowers. I found myself liking him. I smelled not hothouse roses but leather until he began talking about
guns with a heavy sucking of his breath that had re-
placed the "wows." He now made a good living raising
vicious dogs trained for the attack.

Three Naked Ladies

FIRST FIGURE: like a comic version of Botticelli's
Primavera they spin around in my earliest notion of
sensuality, two tall Graces and a short pug-faced attendant who cannot follow the graceful steps of the dance.
They cavort in a common back yard, their grassy slope
a millefleur of dandelions and sour grass. Tufts of
milkweed thistle decorate the sky.

The first woman, a Mrs. Cuddy, has auburn hair
glistening with beauty parlor care, large white teeth, a
hearty laugh, eyeglasses, good skin with freckles, a
restless vitality as she twirls across the lawn. In her
other guise she is well dressed, sitting on a sofa — expensive sofa, armchairs and carpeting in this scene.
Mrs. Cuddy is chattering with visitors. Her house is
semirich Fairfield, but bland pale blue, innocuous rose
prints, a contrived pleasantness. My mother and Mrs.

Cuddy are not really friends but some distant family connection has brought us here on a Sunday. The husband, Mr. Cuddy, who looks like Senator Robert Taft of Ohio, is successful at whatever he does — pudgy face, whitish, unathletic, excessively neat and honest.

In his plaid golf shorts and knee socks he serves drinks while his daughter, his beloved daughter, brings round the crackers and cheese. She is a tight-assed girl who goes to Wellesley and will never marry. At the time of this visit I am supposed to admire her scholastic achievements and social attributes. Janet and her father are a team. With constant attention, clean ashtrays and fresh ice cubes, they keep Mrs. Cuddy sitting. In some way she is their prisoner. Her big laugh escapes across the room. She should be with people who do not fear her energy.

I am curious about Mrs. Cuddy, about her body which is presented to the company with pride. Her hands move about more freely as she talks, yet she is distracted, impatient, and in the moment when she finally rises for a book of matches I can see that she has not really been here with us at all. My petty secret was that I knew her story, had overheard it from the adults some years ago in the holiday gossip. Mr. Cuddy came home to find her in bed with a lover and she ran naked out of the house, out across the neighborhood lawns to a patch of woods where she hid. Her husband covered her with a blanket and brought her in. The word was given out that she was mentally ill. A doctor was found, back in the days when there was only one medical man in Bridgeport who fiddled with the mind. Poor woman, I like to think of her naked running across the grass, not as I saw her pacing the blue carpet of her cage, the roses gone flat on the drapes and walls.

Second Figure: the triumphant woman bejeweled and rosy with the full hips and thighs of the buxom music-hall queen of the nineties is the glorious Mame Rowe. My mother took me to see her a half-dozen times, to a dark-halled old apartment house on the East Side where the neighborhood had all gone Slav and Polish. I believe we brought her money, I don't know, but those trips had a stealthy air about them, and my mother parking the car, pushing the doorbell, wore a look of brave defiance. Buzzed into the gloom of cooking odors and smudged walls we were greeted by Mame herself, poised in the door of her first-floor apartment. Lipstick, rouge, perfume, midmorning earrings — she was a sexy old dame.

"Hi, Loretta!"

"Hello, Mame," my mother said and they gave each other a kiss. That was not my mother's style. She was buttoned-up, demure, yet she did not mind Mame's old silk dressing gown that flapped away from her body as she moved about the dim room.

"You remember Mrs. Rowe, dear?"

Impossible to forget her, white-haired beauty, goddess of illicit love, large, lush, ideal at seventy, ignoring her poverty for she had riches the rest would never know. She stood erect with an ebony cane — it had been the Doctor's, the husband she betrayed. It was for effect, the silk kimono and the cane.

"How's Bill?" she asked my mother.

"Oh, fine."

"They spoiled him," Mame said to me, a playful tough edge to her voice.

My mother agreed. There are no other conversations in my childhood like these. They are all placed in the brown cast of Mame Rowe's apartment.

"His mother and sister," she said. "It was a sin they made so much of him."

Always shy of self-revelation, my mother laughed and told the story about the two apple pies that were baked for my father as a common practice before they were married and he still lived at home — one with nutmeg, one without, to please whatever whim might take him. I don't know why she laughed. She did the same sort of thing: two pies, three shirts pressed by hand as the morning offering.

Mame asked about Rose, my grandmother Kearns who had been her best friend, about Aunt Helen, Leo, Frank, people who hardly spoke to her. Many had dropped her years ago as a scarlet woman, left her to rot for her sin. Well, she did not. Mame made friends with the Czech neighbors, knew their births, deaths, diseases, went to the Polish church, knelt to the same God who forgave her. On election days she got out the vote with her telephone calls for the Democratic ward, the same old raunchy gang of Irish could not refuse her, that's where she came from and the pose of doctor's wife could never have been right.

It was the American success story again: the poor bright boy from the industrial town worked his way through medical school and married the hometown beauty. Dr. and Mrs. James Michael Rowe lived in a roomy house with a broad porch on Noble Avenue, on the fashionable rim of their old neighborhood. Jim Rowe remained my grandfather Kearns's best friend even after my grandfather failed as a labor leader to organize the workers at the Singer Sewing Machine Company and accepted the defeat of a political handout, becoming a county jailer, walking each day to his safe custodial job. Their friendship, that part of the story, was stressed and Rose Kearns got on with Mame. They went to the vaudeville shows. I don't know why it was all so emphatically told to me — their card games, their summer trips. My grandmother Kearns's piano bench was full of the sheet music left from their good times together. The two men were friends: my Grandfather Kearns and Dr. Rowe. Then the Doctor began to drink and Mame took up with another man. The Rowes had no children so Mame went off with a paramour, a dashing Tammany Hall politician, Senator John McCaffrey of New York, and they lived for many years out of wedlock. The Doctor drank, drank away his practice and the house and when she was older Mame came back to care for him. My Grandfather Kearns, whom I never knew, had an attack one night after supper. "Doctor Rowe killed your grandfather": that tale was of mythic proportions. He'd come drunk and with a bottle to the occasion and Grandpa Kearns would have no one to help him but his friend, whom he apparently tried to sober up through the night of his own death. They were in it together to the last.

Rowe fumbled on for a while with a semirespectable job as a public health officer, but the man who killed my grandfather was soon dead of drink. So there was Mame Rowe drawn into her cubbyhole, accepting my mother's handouts with dignity. It was fair exchange:

I've never seen my mother so straight with anyone as she was with this big sexy woman. Each time in that apartment I was given a candy box of jewelry to play with while they talked, gaudy bric-a-brac from Mame's sporting days.

In my mind the story of Aunt Helen connects with the talk between Mame and my mother in that dim brown room. My father's sister was beautiful as a young woman — terrific in her gym suit with the girls' basketball team, a knockout in her studio photo upon graduation from normal school, and my Grandfather Kearns took my mother into Helen's bedroom at night to look at her sleeping, to look at her beauty in repose. It must have been soon after my mother and father were married, when they lived in the flat on Park Street above the Kearnses. My mother, who never spoke an envious word about another woman, hated this adoration of Helen sleeping, said that my aunt was rouged, had made herself up, or worse, had not washed her face for the night. There was something lewd about the mild jailer exhibiting his grown daughter — she, like the little girl of porous alabaster flesh in a Victorian genre painting and he, the gentleman with downcast eyes, all sickly sweet and unaware.

In her heart my mother would not allow it, that she was not beautiful, that her own muted prewar girlishness at thirty-three was less interesting to this family of Kearnses than my aunt's brash twenties style. Well, Helen was — is — a honey. Married and moved the hell out of Bridgeport into one of those army post lives — Frankfurt am Main, Austin, Tokyo, Alexandria, Virginia. Flip and energetic, she always made sport of herself. Europe and Asia viewed from the

vantage point of the Irish East Side. Sleeping beauty
no more. Her quick tongue continued to irritate my
mother. George and I loved Aunt Helen's smart attack
on life as opposed to that reserve my mother pushed at
us too often and too hard.

There is much left unanswered: why at eight or ten
years old I played so docilely with that smudged rhine-
stone jewelry and sprung lockets, junk I hated even
then . . . unstrung beads of lust and faded beauty,
shoe buckles for dancing slippers that were historical
artifacts. On the museum earphones I can hear an
early fox-trot. Mame dances, graceful yet toppling the
tables and chairs of her dark room (so much bourgeois
apparatus). Objects break noiselessly, silk kimono flies
open revealing whalebones, grommets, laces that fall
in a tangle to her thighs. Mame dances, slithering her
flesh-colored harness to the floor. Two steps and a
swoop of the Castle Walk. Now she is naked with the
ebony cane as partner and prop. Mame Rowe, I see
you young as I never managed to see any grown
women, the others all bound in their marriage vows or
spinsterhood. I see you unfettered, blooming fresh
Bridgeport rose in the arms of Senator McCaffrey. No
shame can touch the slope of your ivory stomach to
fair pubic tangle. How surprisingly fine and fair — it
matches the smooth blond hair flung to the winds that
drift through your cluttered and ruined rooms. Grass,
garlands, rose of Sharon nipples. My mother and I sit
tight on the edges of our chairs afluster with Mame's
show of bodily grace. We are united in our bristling
defensive goodness. Is it true no one has ever seen the
real fire in Loretta Burns's hair, or appreciated that her
withdrawal from the physical world is a ploy? Where is

the man to coax her, not bully her back? Someday I
will leave my drunk doctor and go with my love to
New York.

When she knew she was dying Mame Rowe sent me
the old candy box of jewelry, stones missing from rings
and brooches, single earrings, safety clasps gone. My
mother hated that debris: with the grand figure laid to
rest she feared that something of Mame's racy life
might rub off on me and she pitched it all out.

Third Figure: Peggy and I stood for a moment in the
doorway of her room. Across the hall her aunt and
uncle's bedroom door was left open for the breeze.
Two naked bodies passed out on the bed, a man and a
woman, more or less. These were our early teen-age
days when my friend and I laughed uncontrollably at
anyone, a man with a wen on his neck, a neighborhood boy in a goofy baseball cap, a dressed-up lady
with her slip showing. We did not laugh at her naked
aunt and uncle. I must have suppressed a gasp but in
the manner of a best friend she picked it up — "That's
nothing. They do it all the time."

We closed the door to her room. Here she was bil-
leted for the summer during her own family's misfor-
tunes. That summer of her loss would extend itself into
the school year and she would never go back to the colonial house outside of town with garden walls of Connecticut granite, duck pond, woods. The family gardener, named Vladimir, was the source of
innumerable funny stories as were the various "colored
maids" and the Yankee neighbors. Peggy's public manner trembled on the edge of dangerous hilarity. Pri-
vately, she had a reverence for the distinction her fa-

ther had attained. She knew the labels in her clothes
were good. She knew the French pottery they ate
lunch off was *moutarde*, unheard of by most of Bridgeport, and she knew it was classy not to let on. She
cherished the cozy window seats and screened porches
of her home and the sacred vision of her mother, a
selfish indomitable woman, stretched out with undiag-
nosed illness on a chaise longue, reading another mystery. Her four brothers were older, brilliant, known for
charming their way out of trouble with shopkeepers
and traffic cops. Girls worshipped them for their glistening good looks and white tennis clothes and for
their heartbreaking dismissal of local society. They
were slated to be our Kennedy boys.

Peggy, last of the Shea clan, was a chubby, freckled
girl with a cast in her eye. Given to allergies, she often
wore clownish white cotton gloves over raw unhealing
fingers, the subject for much of her own laughter. Our
self-contempt went deeper than our mockery of the
world: anything could set us off — my blackheads or a
clumsy drip of ice cream down a clean shirt. We ached
with laughter at my hammer toe and again when she
knelt in the wrong pew next to a spastic girl after
Holy Communion.

The guest room where she was farmed out that summer was plain with a cast-off double bedstead, clean
muslin curtains, an extra room in the house of a child-
less couple. Her uncle, Michael Shea, was considered
a failure. Off the boat from Ireland before the First
World War on the same day as Peggy's father, Mike
had lost his brogue and native wit. I never saw him
when he wasn't smiling nervously and shuffling the old
jokes around. Michael Shea never got a grasp on life in

America. Mere respectability was a daily chore. Sober
during the day, he worked checking supplies for Whe-
lan Drugs, driving from Stratford to Fairfield to Easton
to Monroe to gather orders for the wholesalers of
shampoo, toothpaste, novelties and paper products.
Now he lay naked next to his stubby wife. Their soft
bodies, indulged in Four Roses and her famous angel
food cake, were drained of sex.

Peggy's dresses hung in the closet of her uncle's
house. Her calamine lotion to soothe her peeling
fingers was set on the dresser, but this was not her
room in any way. It looked out over the back yards
where Parrott Avenue lots joined French Street, over
the cellar hatchways and pulley clotheslines. We never
came here for our continuous conversation, naturally
preferring the cool empty rooms of my grandmother's
house. In haste we took whatever it was we needed that
summer night from Peggy's room and averted our eyes
from that bed like a tomb, husband and wife laid out
for the numb years. For once the giggles that rescued
us from any serious response to the world failed. Our
dreams as we constructed them for each other that
night were not quite intact. Sitting up on the cool
stucco parapet of my grandmother's porch, it seemed
that it might not be as easy for me to lose weight, that
the tall loping boy who spoke to me once on the North
End bus would not fit into my cheap novelette and ask
me to . . . We had always believed, too, that the cor-
rective glasses would draw Peggy's errant eye into line,
that some solution would be found to the problem of
her suppurating hands and sudden hives. The naked
bodies on the bed were the only secret she had kept
from me.

There were signs now that Peggy would not go home in the fall. Her father, an enchanting man referred to professionally as a financier, came alone to visit her on Sundays with no more than a humble quart of ice cream in his hand. Overnight his suits looked worn, the big car less important. The rumors of Shea's downfall had started: Vladimir, the gardener, and the duck pond were all gone. My parents were somber and evasive so I never knew whether it was a simple bankruptcy or whether the darker stories of embezzlement were true. One Sunday we had packed the car to go to Fairfield Beach late in August and drove to the corner. The Beardsley Park bus stopped square in front of us and there was Phil Shea, scrambling off the high step, come to visit his daughter empty-handed.

"I suppose he still has carfare," my father said, kindly enough.

Then Peg and I were not close anymore. Of course we continued to make up our love lives and like true friends described our menstrual cycles. Predictably, she had cramps and just as predictably she found it a howl. Peg now openly idolized her brothers: one, an original mind, would become our next Edison; the scientific brother who had had a touch of meningitis, she saw as half Byron, half Einstein, dragging his foot through the halls of academe; the youngest and most spoiled of the boys she reformed to a priest; and the best-looking Shea became, in fact, a lieutenant in the army, romantic enough in uniform to need no further invention.

Phillip Shea, deflated, aging quickly, fluttered over small domestic errands that took him constantly in and out of the flat they rented on Iranistan Avenue. For

some reason I'm not happy that in this instance I resort
to the literary reference: at home he shuffled the rooms
in slippers, tieless, pants drooping, a perfect Hurstwood
out of *Sister Carrie* while his wife went out magnificently to earn a living as an exalted social worker, dining with state officials, hospital boards and fund raisers.
The woman who was seldom well enough to get off the
chaise longue and come downstairs for lunch went
from strength to strength, thrived on her husband's
failure. Laughing still (now the laughter always came
in the wrong places), Peggy said her mother was incredible, an incredible woman. Mrs. Shea was as tall
as her tallest son, her features as imposing as a handsome man's. To replace her servants she employed her
family: her husband in the kitchen as the cook, Peg
pressing her clothes like a lady's maid and the only son
left at home chauffeuring her to meetings and useful
social occasions in their stripped-down Ford.

The story that Peggy held to all through high school
was the bravery of her father, going back to a heroic
formula. "Just imagine. He came off the boat from
Ireland with twenty dollars and his brother to look
after. Imagine what he accomplished." Laughter,
always too much laughter to undercut any challenge to
her loyalties. Too funny for words, how generous her
father had been. An absolute stitch, the time Igor Si-
korsky or Jim Farley came to dinner. "Just imagine,"
Peggy said. She had lengthened out. The freckles
faded. Her bone-rimmed glasses, only for reading,
were satiric in effect and stylish. The boys who took
notice of her from the Jesuit prep school could not understand what was so hilarious. She was not laughing
at them: it was just imaginable (or unimaginable) that

her father, that Titan of the American business scene, had gone on several occasions to Hyde Park with a lot of rich Democrats — Eleanor Roosevelt in riding breeches with those teeth: it was a riot. Just imagine — her father, sweet evocation of a man (barfly now, pilfering his beers out of the grocery money), met her mother on a society weekend in *Newport*. Her mother was Scotch Presbyterian. Couldn't you just die laughing?

It was as easy to imagine as the luscious plot of a best-seller of the forties . . .

His powerful shoulders strained the seams of his linen jacket as he took the binoculars from her and looked out to Narragansett Bay.

"Do you sail, Mr. Shea?"

"I've gone out for cod, miss, in the Irish Sea," he said, thickening his brogue, "but I've not sailed for pleasure."

"Then, I'll go out with you tomorrow," she said, "for pleasure." They looked out at a sloop neither one of them gave a damn for. "Take me sailing, I'm the poor cousin here. I've nothing to lose."

Peggy sustained herself on such nonsense for years. Peaceable stories, before the fall. We went our separate ways, to different schools. The Sheas prospered enough to send her to a third-rate Catholic college that prepared their girls to be Catholic wives and mothers. At Christmas and Easter vacation she still laughed wildly: sensible grown-up talk about her chemistry courses and double dates would erupt into our old adolescent giggles. Life continued to be too ridiculous — the blast from the Bunsen burner, the graduate student from Boston College who wanted her to . . .

There were no distinctions: sex was a scream on the order of white socks with a dark business suit or the nun with a lisp in theology class.

When the breakdown came she was working in New York. It was violent — Bellevue, then months in a psychiatric hospital in Hartford. In the summer Peggy called when I was home — home being the word I clung to for the stucco house on North Avenue. She insisted on coming to pick me up in the family car and we went out to drink beer in a collegey bar near the Jesuit university where the boys looked like cub scouts to us now. She was tall as her mother, thin, and she'd darkened her hair to mysterious henna. Her clothes were perfect New York. Therapeutic measures, but she was lovely, the new Peg — and there were no laughs.

"I attacked my mother. I screamed at her when they came to take me to Hartford. I threw a chair at her. Can you believe it?"

"Sure, I believe it. So do you."

"I'm glad my father's dead. He had enough."

The score was bad: the four sons — each one seedy and unsuccessful — now Peggy rehabilitated to a solemn beauty. The bar was noisy, I remember, so we talked for hours in the car, serious material we'd never covered.

"We have to think about sex," she said.

I blamed our mothers — hers, the imaginary invalid on that chaise longue with stacks of Agatha Christie; mine, a kitchen Bernini, carving Mary, Joseph, camels and lambs out of the large-size Ivory Soap. Damn them, they never told us anything we needed to know. I remember saying that the man I slept with in the city was good, kind, sweet but we didn't need each other.

(He would march in Selma and on the Pentagon. Last year he sought peace in Belfast with the IRA.) Except late at night on weekends and somewhat drunk, we were not consumed with passion: in the morning we were decorous.

She said: "I had my breakdown in Penn Station." It was too dark in the car to see her new oval face, but she must have smiled at this. "I'd met a boy who was from this rich family . . . you can't imagine."

Yes, I could imagine as she told me all too heavily of the recognizable breakfast room, cosy window seats, perennial border with lupins, delphiniums and bleeding heart. The boy loved her. Perhaps his family had employed a gardener named Vladimir. She was home free, the glamour of her early years was there for the taking. Like a princess come back from exile to find, improbably, the same lamp glowing by the bed, the familiar sheets turned down for her to sleep.

"But he was Protestant," she said earnestly. "We argued about the Trinity."

"Peg, you can't be serious."

"He was *Republican*. How could I?"

"You're crazy."

"Yes. I know."

A small circle of houses, eight or ten, cheap, out of commuter range, halfway out on the South Shore of Long Island. Nowhere, off the highway. Bare sticks of trees, a great show of cement foundation, courageous attempts at self-expression. Here a colonial porch light sways. There a New Orleans grillwork post presents a galvanized aluminum mailbox. Prim white picket, lolling post and rail, aggressive chain fence. Her house was sensibly plain. The kitchen gleamed over a work counter into the living room where the Christmas tree crowded the furniture into unlikely corners. It was New Year's Eve and I had stopped by in the afternoon on my way to Easthampton. My daughter zipped into her snowsuit had slept all the way from the city. Now she stood bewildered in front of the strange toys that sat properly under the tree. Peg's obedient, mirthless children began to play with her like a new doll.

We talked about the local school system and childhood diseases. It was effortless as though she still lived next door. Her glasses were back in place and she was broad from childbearing. She baked every day and brought out a frosted high ring cake. I gave her a bottle of good wine I'd meant to bring to dinner.

"We never drink — only beer." She laughed at that: it was normal self-amusement. Her husband was a strict Catholic. I'd come early that day to avoid him: he disapproved of so much. I refused to subject myself to his pity — the spectacle of me driving out to the fashionable end of the Island like a gypsy, alone with my kid, in a battered Karmann Ghia. He resented any show of style, doggedly clinging to the worthy poverty of his past. His managerial post with the Suffolk Hydraulic Company had not freed him from a narrow blue-collar sensibility. Their house was full of meaningless regulations. Money-saving coupons were clipped from the local paper. Prayers said. Punishment meted out. Nothing was bought "on time." He was a Republican. All dreams were budgeted. This square, clean house cemented into its flat lot could never blow away.

"Don't they have the most awful New York accents," Peg said of her own children. It was obvious that she loved them, that it would never matter to her that they wore cheap clothes from the highway bargain mart and wanted to march in the band for Our Lady of Precious Blood. How we would have giggled ourselves sick at their sort, hidden up on my grandmother's porch.

"This cake was the one my aunt made," Peggy said. "Bridgeport angel food. You know they were good to take me in. They didn't know beans about the care and feeding of children. Oh, God," she started to laugh insanely. Her children turned to her, amazed. "Oh, God," stopping for breath, "do you remember her little round body on the bed?"

"The two of them." I laughed for no reason.

"I only remember her little naked body, just imagine — drunk every night."

Snow was forecast and the first holiday dead announced over the car radio. She had urged me to stay and have a glass of "my" wine when her husband got home. It was easy enough to say I wanted to get on the road before the storm. I would rather have driven through a blizzard that year than confront the man she had married. He would be hearty and smug and make my freedom for all the pain it cost me seem paltry. Their holiday evening — I could fill in that scene with all the facile contempt of a smart-ass liberal filmmaker:

The children are allowed their half-hour of extra television and a piece of Bridgeport angel food. After they have said their prayers the lights of the Christmas tree are unplugged, but the TV remains on throughout as a background until midnight. The images follow of Lyndon Johnson, a Vietnamese child, a reporter from the Golan Heights and grotesque shots of old people in party hats making fools of themselves, jammed onto the dance floor of the Roosevelt Hotel for "Tip Toe through the Tulips," "Sleepy Lagoon," "It Had to Be You."

Peggy, a grown woman bearing a child's name, is somewhat aloof. She maneuvers her large body with skill from the kitchen to couch. In the niceness of her gestures, her distracted nods, smiles of disinterest, we are given the fact that this is our heroine. Of course she hates her end-table lamps with gilt shades, the blue-flowered chair and the crimes of our government. The plot seemingly thickens, but is based on the shallow water of our conditioned response.

Eating cocktail peanuts, she wipes the salt off her hands, then down the sides of her skirt. Her eyes, one quicker than the other, wander to the television set as she listens to her husband. She puts on big owl glasses and turns to him. He is a boorish man, smoothly bald with rimless eyeglasses and bright boyish cheeks — talking about the year to come. Their medical benefits will be increased as of January 1. Coverage for optical examinations and outpatient X rays for dependents. . . . He sounds as though he has ingested the insurance company brochure. Peggy smiles but has nothing to ask him. She brings in the bottle of wine, two glasses, a plate with crackers and a soft heap of cheese the color of orange juice with bloody streaks. Stumped by the corkscrew, her husband stops talking. She opens the bottle.

"She's probably got a boyfriend out there," he says looking suspiciously at the wine label.

Peggy does not answer and they sit side by side eating peanuts and cheese. There is a split screen: Times Square with young fools merrymaking in a cold drizzle / the old smoothies of the orchestra. The countdown is begun: two minutes, one — her husband puts his arm around Peggy and she pulls away to fill the wine glasses — thirty seconds. They kiss. Her head rests safely on his shoulder. Slumped together they watch the replay of the important moment gone. Again they kiss. He is businesslike in his ardor until with a trembling laugh she gently reminds him of the date.

They practice birth control by the rhythm method, ordering their pleasure by the calendar. He spreads cheese on a cracker — from the way they eat and drink it is not clearly indicated whether they will be careless or play it safe tonight.

I spent that New Year's with Jean Stafford Liebling, out in her orderly house. Friends of hers came to dinner, a serious couple who were going on to a serious New Year's Eve party and kept track of the time. During dinner my daughter played upstairs in Jean's study. Through a grating that no longer functioned she sent us drawings and dangled messages on strings into our dinner plates. We wrote back: "Bad girls go to bed." "Happy New Year, Punk." In the middle of the table the lazy Susan turned with mustard, horseradish and that priceless bottle of wine, never to be opened, with a zany fake label (extravagant château, *grand cru* squiggle) that Saul Steinberg drew for his friend shortly before Joe Liebling's death.

My daughter was put to sleep. The serious people went off and we sat for what was left of the year avoiding summaries and predictions, attempting to make the night like any other, but I remember we were not clever and there was no rancor or bitterness in anything we said. We drank nothing much and at five after twelve called it quits. Nothing sorrowful: I had gotten through. Jean, scrubbing over the last pot, dismissed me, a gruff and uncommonly good friend. Upstairs, I lay down in the twin bed opposite my daughter.

In the morning we left early to visit my mother in Bridgeport. It had, in fact, snowed during the night, not at all the disaster predicted, but a gentle inch covering the flat yards and winter hedges of Easthampton. We drove down to the town beach, Loretta in a terrible excitement to see where she had played all summer. At last we had the place to ourselves and there for the first time we saw the sand covered with snow, the sun like a distant Eucharist in the sky, and the frigid beauty of the winter Atlantic.

Documents I

By UNZIPPING the white net evening dress and pulling the childish puff sleeves down off my shoulders, propping up my breasts, I was Natasha. Silk flowers off an old hat in my hair. Seed pearls or the bowknot lavaliere — sometimes I preferred my throat bare. I don't know the exact year in which, all summer long, I read *War and Peace*. The Victorian dresser that now stands in the hallway of my apartment was then in the best bedroom where my grandmother slept. It was in that oval mirror with its machine-turned furbelows and knobbed finials that I watched myself get ready for the ball. Frisky chubette turns fragile darling. I had my choice of several old fans, kid gloves that were yellowed and dry, talcum powder on my nose. My heart quickens as I turn my head to the blank wall — there is André.

An ugly rose taffeta dress, a hand-me-down given to me for Miss Comer's social dancing classes, fell from the shoulders naturally and with a tug displayed everything I had above the nipples, but Natasha wore white.

In college I read the long sections of *War and Peace* dealing with the Masonic brotherhood and Napoleon's march on Moscow for the first time.

IN THE PACIFIC, Charlie lay out on the airstrip and smoked grass. The safest place to smoke on base was the end of the runway. He was a tough smart guy who I like to imagine is still living off the GI Bill from the Second World War. And Christ, not only was he worthless but too old for me, a wizened thirty, but cute. When he wasn't conning the government out of a college education he lived with his aunt, a hacking husk of a woman with platinum hair who chain-smoked and drank blended whiskey while watching the wrestling matches on television.

It was the summer before I went away to college. I had done everything right. Honors. Taken the prom seriously. Delivered the prize-winning speech at graduation.

"No fuck," Charlie said, "you told them about the future."

He was an expert on Proust and Sarah Vaughan. We hung around his house drinking beer and playing records. Sometimes punchy Jack O'Connor, his only friend, would drive us to the beach. In the morning my mother laid Scotch plaid material out on the dining room table to make skirts for me to take to college.

We shopped for sweaters to match. Then I lied and said I was going to a girlfriend's house and went and found Charlie. He took money off me. He stole from his aunt. Charlie had no plans. He had lived in Mexico — that was a possibility. Out in the Pacific he had hepatitis and gonorrhea. Being shiftless he loved warm climates.

I filled out my application for a single room in a large dormitory at Smith. On the map the building was set at the top of a green quadrangle.

"Eighty-seven girls," Charlie said. "Shit — you are going to have fun with those girls."

Once in a fit of decency he sold his blood and actually took me out on a date. With a polite face he came to the house in a sport jacket. My grandmother sat all in black clutching her cane, hunched like a picture-book witch, white hair in a bun, mumbling, blind, bloodless, near death.

"Christ, you are a real old lady," Charlie said. "Look at those wrinkles. Jesus, look at her hands."

That night he had borrowed a car. We listened to Coleman Hawkins at the Tip Toe Inn. On the beach we sloshed the top half of our Cokes out of the bottle and poured in Ronrico rum. Feeling my thighs he said he would never touch me. He predicted that I would go to Smith and wear a polo coat, knee socks. Shit, I was going to have fun with all those girls. I was going to read Thomas Mann and Joyce and go to football games in the Yale Bowl.

"You are going to marry some smart guy," Charlie said, "and even the goddamn hair on his chest will grow in a Y."

A few days after our date Charlie found a ride going west.

IN THE CASE OF Harrison Palmer III it was established by long-distance phone calls and urgent letters that we were in love. Florentine wallets and French perfume were exchanged. He was rich. On the outskirts of New Haven, against university rules, he kept a gray Buick convertible with red-leather seats. We drank daiquiris and ate expensive meals. Bored with his clubby friends we drove into New York and went to the opera or Carnegie Hall. We went to see the pictures his family had given to the Metropolitan Museum. I waited in the car while he checked in with his broker. I was taken to Sutton Place to meet his family. They were mighty classy people who picked up the goblets in which the fruit cup was served and drank down the juice. Harrison's white mouse, named Hugo, escaped down the side of the building into the park and was brought back by the doorman. Mr. and Mrs. Palmer were deeply concerned about the health of the doorman's wife.

Harrison was a virgin, proud of it yet tortured by the fact. During the week he wrote me long letters from New Haven that were passionate and obscene. He further wrote that he was a dedicated rebel. I must never think that it was just the idiots from prep school or the burden of his family's reputation that brought on his

despairing moods. Religion and politics, all the stric-
tures of society were more than he could bear. He was
a true pagan, not a naughty child, and he feared what
might happen to the world once he let himself go.
When he came to meet my parents in Bridgeport he
was charmed by such simple folk. Harrison's gifts grew
more lavish, jewelry and clothes. I knew we had problems in the spring term when those fat letters arrived
from New Haven and I resented the time it would take
from my studies to read about the evils of a corrupt society that oppressed his free spirit, about my armpits
like translucent petals and my pearly nates. He had an
odd fix on the god Pan: I was still somewhat enchanted
by this whimsical rich boy but now I doubted his
goatish half.

A private policeman in a sentinel box waved us into
the town on the Connecticut shore where his aunt and
uncle lived. All the big insurance company money in
America gathered in a private community on one point
of land. On the veranda of a shingled mansion we
were served drinks by Maggie, Nora and Mary, Irish
girls grown old in service. Katharine Hepburn flew in
on a private plane with Howard Hughes. "Kate's
home," they said, but did not bother to turn in their
wicker chairs to see her walking down the beach. They
talked of sailing and tennis, of ranches out West and
skiing in Switzerland. These were the people who troubled Harrison's soul, these ruddy men and smooth
women who hardly bothered to snub me.

After dinner we went out in the Buick. At great
length he talked of his desire for me. It was presumed
when we drove up to the house, by the aunt and the

last of her guests, that we'd been screwing in some boathouse or barn. In the morning Harrison Palmer came into my room to get me up in time to go to Mass with the Irish maids.

IN THIS COLLEGE TOWN in the shadowy Berkshires Oriental rugs and antiques were agreed upon unless you had the money for Eames chairs. Few did. Mostly, people drank together in nice houses and let desire sog into blurry but tender extramarital kisses. The pretty old lady with an excellent body was drunk, waltzing in her living room with a young member of the English department, homosexual. She, who had danced with Martha Graham on the great European tour of '46, crashed into the table, a Mies van der Rohe. A green crack shot through the thick glass. Though it looked like a fresh running stream, she was inconsolable. "Oh, my husband. My husband," she cried, speaking of the retired mathematician, once mildly heterosexual, whom she had married. "Oh, my husband will kill me," she cried pressing the young man to her.

IT WAS HELD as a certainty (how the hell would any-one know) that the couple who were to divorce violently, after not speaking to each other for an entire academic year, had in fact screwed each night, silent and angry.

"Ask her if she wants another drink," he said in the kitchen.

"He told the children he's trading in the car," she said in the living room. It was exciting for them: they were not young but were both energetic and had been living in a fine old house with big bay windows and shade trees for years. They had seen the Berkshire hills, softly molded by time, yet menacing, set at the dead end of town, as though out of a Hawthorne story they'd read too closely. They were the subject of much gossip for a while.

Two Philosophers

To BEGIN WITH it was odd when the two philosophy professors took me with them to the end of the one short commercial street with low wooden shops and one brick bank. There in a gray clapboard building, small as a nasty neglected dollhouse, they visited Norma. I had heard about her from the philosopher who lived downstairs, the senior partner of this firm: I had seen a frightened dark beauty from a distance at a chapel concert.

With a break for their teaching duties or meals, the two men were inseparable, together from early coffee until the last beer often at one or two o'clock in the morning. I met them as I went downstairs to take out the garbage or get the mail. I had no child and sat in the apartment above them reading Dickens, George

Eliot, Hardy. I typed the third and fourth drafts of my husband's dissertation. Sometimes I acted in the college theater up on the main street, playing Masha in *The Three Sisters*, the whore in *Camino Real*, Nora in *John Bull's Other Island*. As yet I did not feel like an idler, but I would gladly let the philosophers draw me into the room where they sat with coffee mugs or cans of beer.

"What do we mean when we say this table is beautiful?"

"Do we say what we mean when we say that this table is beautiful?"

They were pushing all that year out of moral philosophy into aesthetics. The older man, a Don Juan of local fame, was puffy, handsome, restlessly pacing the floor. With a sincerity that even he believed in, he manipulated men and women alike. His eyes tracked me down no matter what sloppy sweater and skirt left from college I'd been reading in upstairs. With a runny nose or bronchial cough, wan with my monthly period, I was his prey — my breasts, navel, crotch, then his ironic smile and the brutal confrontation I might have come for was over.

"An observation always presupposes the existence of some system of expectation."

I took the philosophers in hour doses, like a class. Our circular probing games were not ultimately serious. The younger man, Walt, was unhappily married and so wrenched by tender feelings for his children. He accomplished almost nothing for he lived in a continual state of anxiety, often calling his wife and saying he would not be home.

"Isn't it more accurate to say that I perceive this table to be beautiful?"

Where they found Norma I don't know, but there she stood in her grease-yellowed kitchen, perfectly dressed as though for lunch at a good New York restaurant. Two babies with food-stained mouths and snotty nostrils clung to her skirts. One had to be older than the other. They both had their mother's curly black hair, her honey skin and brown sorrowing Levantine eyes. All three of them looked like they might cry in the next instant.

There were a few small rooms in the house with metal cots and office chairs. The linoleum floors were strewn with filthy stuffed animals, plastic toys and discarded baby bottles with the dregs of warm orange juice and milk. Though there was no sign of domesticity the smell of diapers was tempered by the faint almond scent of lotion or powder. I had been brought here by my two philosophers under the pretext that Norma needed a friend. I'm sure they partly believed this, but they wanted me to luxuriate with them in their captive woman. Her story, yes — Yes, married to a rich cruel old man — through connections she had fled to this scum house on the rim of the Berkshires. They both loved her and in her fear she was totally available to them.

"I'm pleased to meet you," Norma said. Her voice was airy and sweet. The young philosopher was mooneyed with desire. His awkward body as he sat on a metal kitchen chair actually writhed with sympathy for this beauty in distress. It was the older aesthetician, I

know, who took her at night on one of those cots after
the babies were asleep, unfastened her fine clothes,
bending over her stretched brown nipples for his
pleasure.

Here, as a witness to the past, I am totally biased: I
recall that their intentions seemed evil in showing me
their woman. They had me every morning, pawed my
mind. We were into the Cartesian question: How can
it be that states of mind, feelings, expectations influence the physical movement of our lives and can further control, let us say, our appreciation of music and
the plastic arts?

My downstairs philosopher nailed me in his kitchen-
ette — a kiss because I must need it, then the slap in
the face of his smile.

"Walt likes you very much," he said.

"Good."

"He likes you as a woman."

"I didn't think he liked me as a dog or a car." By our
usual scheme of conjecture and refutation I concluded
that I was to lay his oafish sidekick, thus alleviating any
disputes about Norma. Perhaps under the beautiful
table I would prove myself an exemplary student, con-
taining the thrust of the argument at last.

"Take your hands off me." I went upstairs to type for
my husband. I read the great novels and that spring
played Antigone badly, but with justifiable murder in
my heart, defiant as the guards carted me off to be
buried alive.

When I was down and out he found me, the older
philosopher, of course, Don Juan. I felt that my little

girl clung to my skirt, that my eyes were limpid, melancholic. His wife, who had put up with his antics for so long, worried about me.

"He's a bastard," she said, "but he knows a lot. Talk to him."

He took me to a lesbian bar where he was well known. Nervous, straddling the bar stool, he looked the clients over. "Does this make you feel uncomfortable?" he asked.

"What the hell do you want from me?"

At night he rang my phone in New York every half-hour. I was an emotional cripple for not letting him come to me. Two-thirty. Three o'clock. I took the receiver off the hook. The doorbell rang downstairs at five-minute intervals. At last there was silence but I couldn't sleep.

The rapprochement — we were civilized people — took place a month later at the Algonquin, a dark corner of the bar. I had an hour before going to meet a friend at the Music Box to see Pinter's *Homecoming*. In fear, I drank three martinis straight up. He molested me under the table until I dug into his palms with my nails. Then we smiled and talked about the ballet and a paper he was writing for the Aristotelian Society. When it was time to leave he followed me out to the sidewalk and told me I was pathetic, doomed, no better than trash.

In the lobby of the theater I met a drama critic with one of his many girls. He noted that I was drunk. During the performance I fought my way to consciousness. The stage set was an ominous gray. The play is about a prig, a successful professor who returns to his grimy illiterate home with his wife. The subtext is mysteriously sexual, threatening. The wife, the only woman on-stage, crosses her legs.

"You were a model of hats?" she is asked by a crude man.

"No, a model of the body," she replies and draws her hand up her calf slowly, over her knee slowly, offering herself in that caress.

Let us take for our text, as I did with my two philosophers one day long ago, Gilbert Ryle's *Concept of Mind*: Chapter, "The Imagination": "Much as I imagine things sometimes deliberately so I recall things sometimes deliberately."

Documents II

YES, ABOUT THE YOUNG Frenchman. He sent me the most expensive Christmas card of the Virgin Mary . . . "Avec tout mon amour, Chrétien."

At the dinner party where we met it was a pleasure for me not to find the extra man a divorced overly gay blade. How delightful for him not to have a "possible" girl who spoke college French thrust at him with another meal. I wore a crepe dress, not white but the color of cream. I don't know why I remember that detail, but his well-tailored suit has some significance. He was a stocky young man from a provincial town, thick in the shoulders with sturdy legs. All that Parisian tailoring was a waste.

His English was so-so. I have no French, but before the dessert we had agreed through our gestures upon the course of our evening. The coffee and brandy were waiting it out. In front of our host and hostess we played the following game:

"I weel woke you home," he said.

"It's just a few blocks."

"But pleeze, no trouble."

We even lingered in a neighborhood bar on the way (later I found out it was a homosexual pickup joint, what matter) telling, as best we could, our stories.

"Won't you come up?" I said at my door.

"You have a nize place," he said. "Eez terrible my place."

There was the furniture I'd assembled for this part of my life and a Bokhara rug I'd bought at auction to put down over the rotten wood floors that shaled up under our feet. I had pulled too many slivers out of my daughter's heels and toes. The couch which I'd scavenged from the street was newly covered for a fortune. But I do not want the two of us standing in that first evolution of the Tenth Street apartment to dissolve into caricatures: brave divorcée who has made her nest, good cook and PTA mother, a touch dicey as she pulls off an earring, kicks a shoe: solid young man, not yet hardened to the corporate world that has shipped him overseas, not yet damaged by the glamour of New York. He has some trouble with cufflinks and his tie. Around his thick brown neck is a gold religious medal to protect him from harm. Furthermore, it is comic that we cannot pronounce each other's names. Here I will give no banal erotic scene. Cross out the parody of Charles Boyer and my striving on the page for the inevitable bliss. Leave it that we were inventive. I will not deny us our humanity.

That Christmastime the poet John Hollander came to drink with me, flipped over my Bokhara and pronounced it a steal. As always he was kind, but he was curious to know if, now that I had established myself, there was heartache for the past.

NOTE TO A dissatisfied married friend: It is not true that we would have loved each other if by some fate (how's that for romance) we'd met when you were at Amherst and I was at Smith, a magic seven miles away. You would have loved Miss Rich Bitch who hurt you and I would have continued to scrape my black Irishman, gifted with beauty then, out of the bars of New Haven.

HALFWAY UP THE mountain to the Santa Ynez Pass: Below, the city of Santa Barbara at night, dazzling — strips of light along the Pacific and looping out onto the wharves: the beat of the searchlight sweeping the sky from the airport out on the flatland near the university.

Inside, a birthday party attended by three couples and the fantasy for the evening was formal dress — black tie, champagne. It smacked of a longing for New York, but a New York none of them had lived in, a made-up idea like fine manners.

The blond woman was exquisite. Two strips of black

silk covered her breasts and then tied at the back of her
neck leaving the tanned flesh of her shoulders bare.
Her husband, a lanky Jewish intellectual, had found
her in Seattle — a raw Canadian girl much sought
after. As a teacher she adored him, this childish demanding man who would make her correct her sloppy
thoughts. He threw tantrums when she could not pro-
ceed with simple logic from A to B. It was said that she
had "quite a life" before he took her in hand and did
his Pygmalion on her. Now she was stylish and re-
served, still she kept the habit of smiling too openly at
people and she would look in one direction for a long
time like an animal.

With the champagne there were pâté and witty
presents — Geritol, a prickly cactus like a nightmare
erection and so forth. She seemed to listen while the
others discussed university politics and the overload in
the department of Renaissance men. Her husband had
never managed to get her past the most accessible plays
of Shakespeare, and because she was outrageously
pretty it was said that she was stupid. She was known to
be wonderful with cats and plants. While they argued
theories of revenge tragedy she licked the rim of her
champagne glass and watched the urgent throb of red
signal lights on the runway bring the last plane of the
day from Los Angeles into town.

A fruity white wine was served — Happy Birthday in
this dream world — with Pacific crabmeat rémoulade
atop ripe avocado. Real politics next. There is no dis-
sent. All stand firmly against the war, the university officials, the fascist governor. All support the young
Marxist professor, political prisoners. With the filet of
beef a serious claret and film criticism. Here she lifts

her bare arm from her lap to touch the sleeve of the man next to her. Immediately this is interpreted as a flirtatious gesture. She is somewhat animated, a blond strand escapes over her ear. Her husband has taught her to speak of the deep-focus lens, acceleration, montage, and she spills it out in her soft Canadian burr like a child with news of when the Mississippi was discovered or that the stock market crashed in 1929.

She loves the movies, but they press on to spatiality, nascent motion. Now she is visibly bored with them and hurt. As she adjusts the black silk over her breasts, her nipples harden and she looks down at herself and then out at the life of the city below.

The lengthy pretension of salad and cheese. A scholar (eighteenth-century man) at the university was being demolished as a reactionary, his work destroyed and his person besmirched as puny and squat. A sexual slur was used.

She said: "It isn't true that because a man is short he has a small cock —"

"Yes, my dear," her husband said.

"And some very tall men have small cocks. There are short men with nice thick cocks and neat balls." She was fully alive, glowing, a beautiful woman, and by God she had something to tell them worth knowing: "A good cock needn't be so big anyway," she said.

Yes, my dear, yes, yes, yes.

THEIRS WAS A love match. I always flip back to them, my parents. Though they married late, theirs was not a marriage of accommodation watered down by the waiting. Loretta and Bill, the profanity in my use of their first names. Honor them but never wonder how he laid siege to her, why with all the girls free to go dancing he wanted this lady with her eternal gloves and hats. Cult of the Virgin. Daughter of Virtue. Mother most Holy. So restrained that when she had fun, and she did, it was so proclaimed and labeled *fun*. And that in him which had once been attracted to the rituals of the Church or to the idea of himself as an appealing choirboy: she would iron his shirts when they married and send him off to the courthouse as though in a starched alb. He would be the better for her, quite the little man.

They courted on long walks and ice cream sodas while everyone else drank bootleg booze. Forever after they would tell their children: "We didn't need liquor. Isn't that right, Mother (Dad)?" It was enough to drive me to drink in high school, rye and ginger ale, that picture of them sitting in the Big Top Coffee Shop of the Barnum Hotel slurping their better-by-far chocolate sodas. I see them in the spotlight of her virtue. Children over thirty with the circus-parade mural marching the wall behind them. Where would she have been without his coarseness, his jokes about breaking wind, his foul mouth curbed for her. "Fatty Arbuckle," he said to the waitress's backside. "Piss-elegant" he called her college friends. The running patter of his talk to everyone they met — God, she needed his glibness like his sweat and the hitch of his pants against his balls and in the nick of time there came the engagement ring set in dull platinum which was the fashion. In another instant, with her wide

Celtic cheekbones and narrow chest she would have appeared forevermore in two dimensions, dissolved into her sainthood, one among many in a frieze of virgins.

Miss Burns, the teacher of Latin and algebra, was not supposed to marry and that part of herself, brilliant and stern, which had made her pupils strain beyond their limits she never showed to her husband who was a self-indulgent boy.

The unending text for me of that marriage: their first child dead at birth, then George and . . . while she was showing strangers interested in the economic design of our new 1930's elf cottage . . . her/my water-bag burst and I pressed, inconvenient, difficult from the start, into the world.

FROM BIRTH. At nine o'clock in the morning the panel of sex experts agree upon infantile erections, frequency and delight thereof, but after the commercial break, in which pine forests are brought into the bathroom and kitchen of a studio set to mask any scent of a living creature, they argue over stimulus and response in baby girls. Depending on whether I — I leave the toast crumbs and settle close to the television set — depending on whether I side with Monica Menarche, Ph.D., who has attached electrodes to the clitorises of over five hundred newborn baby girls in the Manhattan area (thereby breeding, at least, a new clinical subdivision of nymphomania) . . . Monica's find-

ings show arousal of the tiny projectile and in some instances even a labial swelling . . . or whether I am
won over by Dr. Max Solemnus, a gray old European
with stunning qualifications in both psychiatry and
gynecology, who dismisses the little female pinprick of
anticipation — "Yah, vile mit der penis . . ." "While
with the penis" — your record is stuck, Dr. Max,
while with the penis over and over is not a statement of
fact. Do not repeat it to me like the ten causes of the
Austro-Prussian War you recited from your varnished
gymnasium desk on the Lundstrasse.

Revisions have been made, Herr Doktor. I am no
longer the victim of your sorrowful wisdom. I repudi-
ate the bruised sacks under your eyes and your drooping nose. Somewhere in your soul you know you
would leave those wired baby girls to die, exposed to
the elements on the East River Drive rather than admit
. . . Take your gloved hand out of me, Dr. Solemnus. Once too often you have said, "This may hurt a
little."

I decide for Ms. Menarche and the proven blips of
pleasure in her infant clitoral readings. She knows less
but she comes up with the answers. Fortyish, starchy
and efficient, she has a decent figure, glasses, the mild
face of a concerned teacher, but a rasping insistent
voice carries her message over the vivacious pleadings
of the panel moderator. Monica, for I'm with her all
the way, has proved the high potential of sexual response in women from crib to coffin. We've got it.
Graphs of gratification.. Samplings of the seventy-five
to eighty group in Hickory Retirement Village. Under
the sympathetic conditions of her well-appointed office
she has cured innumerable men of premature ejacula-

tion and instructed the impotent. Proof positive: Mark
Menarche, her husband, after the birth of Melissa and
again during his career crisis could not sustain . . .
Tell it Monica, all of it — tasteless but so necessary.
Tell how you failed to conceive after thesis and of your
menstrual sadness: lay the measure of your clot and
flow before me. My loyalty will last through the next
commercial break (floorwax).

My mother's delicacy dictated in a whisper that the
box of Kotex be kept in the black reaches of the
bathroom linen cabinet under a mound of unused towels. At the shaded, turreted Academy of Our Lady of
Mercy the nuns all but insisted that my body was on
loan like a library book or a company car. My arms
and legs but above all my womanly appurtenances,
mons veneris, the very curve and tilt of my womb existed for a higher purpose. How many years has it
taken to claim myself — big ass, caesarean scar, broad
hands good for scooping potatoes out of the dirt of
Killarney . . . the mockery, will I ever leave off. All
right: once with small waist, high breasts in that blue
cord suit of mine, size eight, the white ingenue collar
cut low . . . Why all that sludge from the past? I am a
comfortable slut in my bathrobe watching morning
television. I stand firmly against the endless sifting
and measuring of Dr. Solemnus — "Yah, clinikly
shpeegink, but — " Freud has been mishtooken. I admire without question Monica Menarche, the folly of
her enthusiasm, the vulgarity essential to any revolution is also essential to life.

"The voluntary lubrication of the vaginal passage,"
says Monica, "has been fully established from birth."

"From birth?" shrieks the moderator, moderate no

longer. Solemnus nods in sad agreement. Mother of
God, I was ready at birth.

SCENE: A filthy coffee shop that should have flies but
it is not yet the season. The chain hitched to the ceiling is of light-weight brass lacquered to a permanent
shine and from it swings a fat moon-faced watch taken
from the vest pocket of a cheesy giant. The watch
revolves with mechanical accuracy giving us now the
time (eight thirty-five), now the name of a famous
beer.

At Smith the girls from New York in the "creative
writing" class were enamored of a Spry sign on the Pal-
isades that used to flash red across the Hudson and was
most clearly seen in the vicinity of Morningside
Heights. That tacky commercial touch in their stories
meant broken hearts, disillusion and sadness after sex,
though no one, even in this urbane set, ever had
heroines (themselves) fucking in those days. Eyes met,
hands groped up in a Riverside Drive apartment as
love, the real thing, mounted. . . . Fade-out and the
old Spry sign flashed its antiromantic message across
the river.

I find those sophisticated girls were wrong — well, it
was much easier to be brittle at the age of twenty when
wisdom is easily come by. The big watch is merely
comic, as incidental to our scene as the ersatz orange
juice and foul metallic coffee, not worth a sneer and
may be considered a saving distraction revolving the

time and beer while I feel your body on me as though still . . . the whole stretch and lovely weight of you. I've lost my wit. I am quiet — on the theory that reserve about my deepest feelings keeps them fresh. Your penis, exotic and everyday, floats through my mind like an afterimage. Who cares about the cigarette burns in the Formica, the dirty spoon, fluorescent light — eclipse it with a wink. This is as fine for us now as some foreign garden with terra-cotta walls, cool vines and discreet waiters. Look, I'm perfectly happy with the Schlitz sign and the hour. I've finally learned not to want things I cannot have.

THIS PERSISTENT IMAGE: I am walking up Murray Hill to Grand Central, twenty-three years old, soon to marry. It is five o'clock. Early spring. The last golden hour of the day. Next week or the week after may be Daylight Saving Time. This is natural time. Everything in sight is nicely edged, bright: cluttered window of the stationery store, florist display of forced hothouse blooms — both are shops on the ground floor of the building where I work. I cross Madison Avenue against the light, stopping traffic to get to the Morgan Library side of the street. The rose marble of the mansion, everything is clear: within the iron fence the slick dark green of ground cover come to life, the mahogany bushes, vulnerable azalea leaves of pale lettuce green, tulips on the verge . . . this is a memory unlike others: there is no narrative line, nor moral turn. I am

simply walking the blocks to catch my train in a blue
cotton suit with white collar and cuffs, a straw hat, sti-
letto heels. And I am in a state of bliss — wild and un-
accountable. I am beginning. My life is beginning. No
one can stop me.

I charge past the side streets of handsome town
houses, the Polish embassy, the flags of the Dartmouth
and Princeton clubs. All this I construct now — a
hokey social context which distorts the image. It is
unimportant where I come from — the advertising office with indulgent Mr. Lovett who is more embarrassed than angry when he finds me reading *Middlemarch*
instead of typing his dull letters — or, where I am
going — home to Bridgeport on the commuter train,
to the big stucco house with its dwindling family life,
supper on the stove. In particular this moment has nothing to do with the letter I will write to my fiancé that
night, a message in which my longing for him is already shared with dinner plates, toasters, ushers and
bridesmaids.

Years later, trying to capture my transcendent walk
up Murray Hill in a poem, I failed, consigned it to logical time, the past. The faded band of a hat, the cheap
detail of a cracked leather trunk in the attic were a spiritual order to feel regret. I gave the stoplights a false
sexual dimension. No — I am beginning. My life is
beginning (which can't be true) as I walk on in my
New York stride, on in that old Knox hat circa 1918,
dug out of a closet, a musical comedy Peg o' My Heart
boating straw. The theatrical touch, yes, always —
make what you will of it. The sun is glued to the plate-
glass windows of a restaurant in sheets of gold like
blinding insights. I am magnified. The glint of brass

numbers and knobs. Everything is clear. Promise in Rich and Tang Investment Brokers. I am twenty-three, splendidly alone on a city street. A canopy throws an oblong shadow on the pavement at a mysterious angle which I transect undaunted. No one can stop me. Propelled by happiness I hardly touch ground the last blocks and then I come triumphantly to rest on Forty-second Street on the edge of evening and my glorious light dims to the ordinary flat blue of a city dusk.

SINCE THEN I have married twice. Now I love to sit in rooms with the feel of walls about me like a shell or I can look out at the view — there is that choice: to look out at cars, people, trees, the mailman — call it life. Enclosed I can hear the motors and voices, an occasional bark or siren and on a windy day the zing of the black wire's one noted song. Lucky day for me when the wind blows in from Jersey. Or, I can turn as I often do to this room. Here I have put chairs and a table, a soft lamp. Come (I will say) sit with me. Would you like music? I can put a record on, make an omelet. Wine or beer?

Whatever you like. Talk to me. I'll confess that I once loved eggs — to eat, yes, but I mean the perfect shape of them. I have marble, mother-of-pearl, Ukrainian Easter eggs, plastic, opaline — talk to me —ovoid brass paperweights. It was shameful, some female nonsense. They were dead eggs, weren't they? I have an old wooden darning egg — I could mend your socks — and the real turquoise shell of a jay. Pretty but dead. So I swore off. Worse still are my boxes — Florentine paper, abalone shell, Indian bark. That madness of my secrets — stray hairpins, foreign coins, receipts. Don Diego cigar boxes holding what? Buttons, blank spools, the melodrama in a lapel stud with the standard of my father's artillery regiment, the Forty and Eight. Such trash: the poignancy of a baby tooth, an extra set of keys to the Karmann Ghia sold in 1968, the only car I ever loved. Let me give you this Kennedy half-dollar and the cufflinks. Talk to me.

I am twenty-three years old walking up Madison Avenue. No one can stop me. The glorious light dims.

Now, IF YOU WILL step up, Ladies and Gentlemen, to this gaudy nickelodeon in the penny arcade. Put your money away, sir, the show's on me. You will see the death-defying escapades of a man and woman on the high trapeze without a net, the amazing feats of modern marriage. Our aerialists are totally dependent on each other. If for one second — this one's not for the kiddies, madam — if for one second either partner loses his or her concentration it's curtains, Doctor Death. And the easy wrist catch! The single spin! Observe the perfect coordination, the effortless — ah, the thrilling somersault. Silence please! The next acrobatic dare, a triple flip, has never before been attempted in North America. She swings out once, twice. Their timing must be perfect. He hangs by his heels, hands stretched to catch her and one, two, three — ah, she is splattered in the sawdust, a horrible sight. Bring on the elephants. Bring on the band. Peanuts. Popcorn. Candy.

In the next reel we see a honeymoon cottage. The wife is moving about the kitchen in gay, jerky movements, icing a cake, stirring a stew, lighting the candles on a dear table. Up the front path in an exaggerated stagger comes the husband, hat atilt, tie askew, falling in through the front door, shattering a dinky telephone table. He snores on the couch. The little woman dabs at her eyes with the corner of her apron. The candles burn down. He awakes hungry. They kiss and eat in gay jerky movements. Now they are in a restaurant. She is laughing and talking. He is staring, drool-mouthed beyond her. Little does she know that behind her back a big-breasted blond is preening at her husband. She is laughing and talking . . . suspicious, she turns — oho — the spaghetti flies. They fight and make love.

Now there is a baby in a high chair. They move in gay jerky movements picking up toys. How they laugh as the baby sucks noodles. At a party he is talking. She is fox-trotting with a younger man. Pulling and prodding she tries to get her husband up. She is fox-trotting with a younger man. Now the baby is in bed. The husband is reading. See how the wife smiles and turns before him. He is reading. See how she primps and struts the room. This is her new dress. Phooey. He is reading. She pretends she is dancing with a younger man. Next reel is the bedroom, Ladies and Gents, organdy curtains, pretty bedside lamps. He is in floppy

striped pajamas. She is all covered in a flannel
nightgown. Her hair is in curlers and her face shines
with cream. He approaches her with his huge male
member like a blood sausage. Her cunt is like flank
steak. The bed covers move in hilarious jerky
movements.

Now they are in the kitchen. The door is open. Her
husband is drinking. She is laughing too much, stirring and crashing the pots and pans. She is laughing.
Behind the door her lover is crouched in a raincoat
and slouch hat. Ha! Ha! She shoves back the door to
hide him. Her husband is drinking a beer. She is setting out knives and forks. Whew — she shoves back
the door and her lover falls into the room. "Daddy,
Daddy," she cries. Ha! Ha! Now they are walking with
the child between them up the path to the honeymoon
cottage. They turn and wave bye-bye. The door of the
house closes behind them. A ribbon appears held in
the mouth of two turtledoves. It reads: THE END, Ladies and Gentlemen. They fight and make love.

TEN YEARS AFTER the grand passion we sit at a sooty
sidewalk café and find that we are engaged in yet another mistake. One of life's simple-minded ironies
emerges. This is a singles bar. The girls are athletic
with bad complexions, bleached facial hair, breasts
hard as squash balls. The men — all in their late
twenties — are like college boys. They have come on
bikes with their Frisbees and tennis rackets. It is like a

hideous fraternity party at a bad school. Their bodies, all of them, seem pointlessly ugly. There is no tenderness. None.

"We are too old for this."

You say: "We are too young."

The dome of our intimacy descends. You finish my sentences. I repeat that I am fond of the young man you love. We are like perverse children, like fools drinking wine together in the sun and as we walk off we both see, in one instant, three terrible men at a table looking for a piece of the action. They are your age with hair parted low, the strands pasted over their bald heads and gold chains gleam in the gray hair on their chests.

THIS LETTER THEN, written by my father on state of Connecticut stationery. Judicial Department. My mother suffered prolonged attacks of bursitis. On this occasion in the summer we were left with her and my Grandmother Burns at a resort outside Holyoke, Massachusetts. Mount Jefferson House: a rambling, rundown firetrap full of uppity Boston Irish. The food was hearty. The jokes clean. This letter then, written by my father to my mother: that ill-matched pair.

Monday PM

Dear Loretta:

I had a long wait for my train. It was on time but there were hundreds of servicemen returning to New York vicinity. The train was crowded. I went immediately to the dining car. Not that I was really hungry but it was a pleasant place to sit. Much to my surprise my railroad pass was honored so I paid no fare. The train was late on arrival in Bridgeport. I got a bus after purchasing a Sunday Post and after reading it went to bed.

I was up early this morning. Went to Burns Co. and got a favorable report on last week's work. Tell Grandma that everything went splendidly. This morning I looked at your garden and definitely the tomatoes will not be ripe until next week. I already have a "lost" feeling as it were. Two or three times I found myself unconsciously going to call you by phone at home. I went to the bank this morning and sent off the interest check.

It is warm here today and it being about four o'clock I think I will find some business at the Fairfield Police station and take in a swim. You would never guess what I will do then? If Matty has any "dogs" I will have my lunch there.

Be sure and admonish George and Maureen to tell you when they leave the house. Get George to bed at night. I used to get him no later than 9:30 or 10 o'clock. How is his cold I wonder? And your arm. Please use it sparingly and get out in the sun. Be careful not to get sun burned.

Please dear do not worry about anything at home or me. Tonight I will probably see Pat Deady and after talking to him for a while will get to bed. Give both the children a big hug and kiss for me and you my dear take X X X X and X X X X X and X X X X X

Lovingly,
Bill

There are ten more such kisses. The stamp is gone, but the cancellation — Buy War Bonds — remains. The postmark is Aug. 9, 1943. He would have been forty-nine years old and my mother fifty-three.

I AM WALKING UP lower Madison Avenue in an old straw hat, circa 1918. Yes, always the heightening. The last golden hour of the day. Everything is clear: the rose marble of the Morgan Library, mahogany bushes, tulips on the verge. Soon to marry, I am twenty-three years old in a blue suit, size eight. Natural time. I hardly touch ground the last blocks to Grand Central, but come triumphantly to rest alone on Forty-second Street, on the edge of evening. I am beginning. My life is beginning which cannot be true.

FOR THE BEST IN PAPERBACKS, LOOK FOR THE

In every corner of the world, on every subject under the sun, Penguin represents quality and variety—the very best in publishing today.

For complete information about books available from Penguin—including Pelicans, Puffins, Peregrines, and Penguin Classics—and how to order them, write to us at the appropriate address below. Please note that for copyright reasons the selection of books varies from country to country.

In the United Kingdom: For a complete list of books available from Penguin in the U.K., please write to *Dept E.P., Penguin Books Ltd, Harmondsworth, Middlesex, UB7 0DA.*

In the United States: For a complete list of books available from Penguin in the U.S., please write to *Dept BA, Penguin*, Box 120, Bergenfield, New Jersey 07621-0120.

In Canada: For a complete list of books available from Penguin in Canada, please write to *Penguin Books Canada Ltd, 10 Alcorn Avenue, Suite 300, Toronto, Ontario, Canada M4V 3B2.*

In Australia: For a complete list of books available from Penguin in Australia, please write to the *Marketing Department, Penguin Books Ltd, P.O. Box 257, Ringwood, Victoria 3134.*

In New Zealand: For a complete list of books available from Penguin in New Zealand, please write to the *Marketing Department, Penguin Books (NZ) Ltd, Private Bag, Takapuna, Auckland 9.*

In India: For a complete list of books available from Penguin, please write to *Penguin Overseas Ltd, 706 Eros Apartments, 56 Nehru Place, New Delhi, 110019.*

In Holland: For a complete list of books available from Penguin in Holland, please write to *Penguin Books Nederland B.V., Postbus 195, NL-1380AD Weesp, Netherlands.*

In Germany: For a complete list of books available from Penguin, please write to *Penguin Books Ltd, Friedrichstrasse 10-12, D-6000 Frankfurt Main I, Federal Republic of Germany.*

In Spain: For a complete list of books available from Penguin in Spain, please write to *Longman, Penguin España, Calle San Nicolas 15, E-28013 Madrid, Spain.*

In Japan: For a complete list of books available from Penguin in Japan, please write to *Longman Penguin Japan Co Ltd, Yamaguchi Building, 2-12-9 Kanda Jimbocho, Chiyoda-Ku, Tokyo 101, Japan.*

FOR THE BEST IN BIOGRAPHY, LOOK FOR THE

☐ **LIFE AND DEATH IN SHANGHAI**
Nien Cheng

Nien Cheng's background—she was a London-educated employee of Shell Oil, and the widow of an official of the Chiang Kai-shek regime—made her a target for fanatics of China's Cultural Revolution. Her refusal to confess to being an enemy of the state landed her in prison for six years. *Life and Death in Shanghai* tells the powerful, true story of Nien Cheng's imprisonment, resistance, and quest for justice.   *548 pages   ISBN: 0-14-010870-X*

☐ **THE FLAME TREES OF THIKA**
Elspeth Huxley

With extraordinary detail and humor, Elspeth Huxley recalls her childhood on a small farm in Kenya at the turn of the century—in a world that was as harsh as it was beautiful.   *282 pages   ISBN: 0-14-001715-1*

☐ **CHARACTER PARTS**
John Mortimer

From Boy George and Racquel Welch to the Bishop of Durham and Billy Graham, John Mortimer's interviews make compulsive reading, providing humorous and illuminating insights into some of the most outstanding characters of our time.   *216 pages   ISBN: 0-14-008959-4*

☐ **GOING SOLO**
Roald Dahl

In this, the acclaimed memoir of his adult years, Roald Dahl creates a world as bizarre and unnerving as any you will find in his fiction.
   "A nonstop demonstration of expert raconteurship"   —*The New York Times Book Review*   *210 pages   ISBN: 0-14-010306-6*
